THE LOST SQUADRON

THE LOST SQUADRON

A TRUE STORY BY DAVID HAYES

A Madison Press Book
produced for

BLOOMSBURY

Bloomsbury Publications
2 Soho Square
London S1VSDE

A CIP catalogue record for this book is available from the British Library

Produced by
Madison Press Books
40 Madison Avenue,
Toronto, Ontario,
Canada M5R 2S1

Printed in Great Britain

To the members,
living and dead,
of the legendary Lost Squadron —
the pilots and crews
of flights Tomcat Green
and Tomcat Yellow

All men dream: but not equally. Those who dream by night in the dusty recesses of their minds wake in the day to find that it was vanity: but the dreamers of the day are dangerous men, for they may act their dreams with open eyes, to make it possible.

T. E. LAWRENCE,
SEVEN PILLARS OF WISDOM

CONTENTS

PROLOGUE

LATE ON THE MORNING OF TUESDAY, AUGUST 12, 1980, a tiny Beechcraft Bonanza painted red, white and blue scudded over Bathurst Island, nearly eight hundred miles north of the Arctic Circle. It was a fine sunny day, a little below freezing. At six thousand feet there was visibility up to fifteen miles and scattered layers of broken clouds below. In the pilot's seat Richard Taylor checked the Bonanza's instruments and made a slight correction to the plane's northeasterly course. Beside him Pat Epps consulted the charts. They'd flown more than three thousand miles in pursuit of a quixotic obsession — to locate and then "roll" (fly upside down over) the North Magnetic Pole.

"You know, Pat," Taylor said, "I've never rolled the Bonanza before. Maybe I should practice it one time."

"Nah," Epps replied. "If you're gonna mess it up, might as well mess it up there as here."

"Guess that's so."

Mess it up. To listen to Epps's southern drawl it sounded as if he was talking about miscalculating the course by a degree or two. When a pilot messes up a roll it can mean going into a violent spin and ending up an FAA accident statistic.

A stocky, clean-shaven forty-six-year-old, Epps was an airplane dealer who operated a hangar at a general aviation airport in Atlanta, Georgia. The Bonanza was his. Two years Epps's junior, Taylor was tall, trim and bearded, an Atlanta architect. They were the kind of men who chafed at the confines of urban America. They'd flown around the Caribbean and South America, through the Bermuda Triangle, to Mexico to visit a gold mine. They'd first tried to reach the pole in 1978, but a nasty engine knock had forced them back. In 1979 Taylor had undertaken a solo flight, but bad weather and a broken radio receiver had made him cut the trip short.

The North Magnetic Pole is a region of magnetic activity that makes compass needles point north. Unlike its geographical counterpart, the pole is not fixed, but drifts. According to Taylor's research, the National Geographic Society placed it at Allard Island, northwest of the Penny Strait. The aviation charts listed it at King Christian Island, one hundred miles farther north. Pilots in the bar at Resolute Bay put it at a third location.

Unwilling to travel so far only to roll the wrong pole, Epps and Taylor flew to all three, calculated the central point between

Richard Taylor (left) and Pat Epps (right) at Sondre Stromfjord in Greenland.

(Above) An iceberg adrift in arctic waters. (Below) Trailing smoke, Epps's Bonanza loops the loop at an air show.

the Bonanza until the speed rose so high that the airspeed indicator touched the yellow caution line. Then they lifted the nose above the horizon and turned the wheel to its limit. The plane began to roll until the clouds were below and the ocean above.

Within about one hundred miles or so of the North Magnetic Pole, compasses become unreliable. Like a lost child the needle wanders listlessly, searching for north. Then, closer to the pole, it stabilizes. The Bonanza's compass stabilized at 330 degrees no matter which direction the plane was flying, even while making a 180-degree turn or during a roll. Epps and Taylor speculated that 330 degrees indicated the magnetic field of the airplane itself.

them and then made for that point.

Below them the ocean was a rich blue green — lapis lazuli cut with emeralds — filled with broken ice floes that glittered like diamonds. Brown islands — tundra turned to a brackish mud in the relatively balmy summer temperatures — were visible in the distance.

"Think this is it?" Epps asked.

"Guess so," Taylor replied.

"Okay, then..."

Epps and Taylor take their adventuring seriously. To this day they have told no one, not even their wives, who rolled the pole first. Each took a turn lowering the nose of

Their mission accomplished, Epps and Taylor shook hands, cracked open a couple of Cokes from their cooler and returned to Resolute. On the tarmac Taylor excitedly told a maintenance worker that they had rolled the pole. "Uh-huh," the man replied. "How much fuel you want?"

Oh, well. Their friends and relatives in Atlanta would be more impressed by their

After they'd rolled the pole, Epps and Taylor flew from Resolute Bay to Pond Inlet.

achievement. Having been away for four days, Taylor said, "Well, Pat, I'm ready to go home."

"I want to go to Narssarssuaq."

Taylor's eyes widened. In 1977 he and Epps and two friends had flown a twin-engine plane from Atlanta to Europe to attend the Paris Air Show. They had intended to refuel at Narssarssuaq, a famous World War II air base nestled in mountains at the end of three parallel fjords on the southern tip of Greenland. In aviation circles it was considered a legendary approach.

On the day they arrived, a thick blanket of fog and clouds obscured everything but mountainous peaks. Then Taylor spotted the base through a narrow break in the clouds. Dive through that hole, he told Epps, who was flying at the time, but the more cautious Epps kept circling and finally flew on to another airport.

Taylor had never let him forget it.

"That's fifteen hundred miles out of our way, Pat," he said now.

"I'm going back to make that approach."

"No, man, that's crazy."

"It's my plane, and that's where I'm going."

They flew that afternoon to Pond Inlet, a settlement on the northeast coast of Baffin Island. The next day they crossed the Davis Strait and spent the night at Sondre Stromfjord on the west coast of Greenland. Sitting in the hotel bar they took a ribbing from a group of Danish pilots and airport staff — a crowd that one might assume had seen everything, but who couldn't believe a couple of good ol' southern boys were buzzing around the Arctic in a single-engine plane on what sounded like a lark. The pilots talked about crash landings and how to survive afterward in the harsh arctic environment. Then the conversation turned to planes lost on the ice cap, and someone mentioned the Lost Squadron — six P-38 fighters and two B-17 bombers that ditched on the ice cap in 1942. The airport manager said they had been visible on the surface as recently as the early sixties.

That's a coincidence, Taylor thought. A couple of years before, a pair of Atlanta-based commercial pilots named Russell

After landing at Godthaab in Greenland, Epps and Taylor flew south along the rugged coast of Greenland.

Rajani and Roy Degan had approached Epps about using his hangar to reconstruct some warplanes they were planning to salvage from Greenland. Epps told them that wasn't his line of work, but added that he'd flown over Greenland the previous year. Rajani and Degan hadn't been north, and they'd pored over his snapshots like a couple of kids.

The next day Epps and Taylor continued south to Godthaab, Greenland's capital, and from there to Narssarssuaq. The final 250-mile flight took them over a dramatic coastline featuring some of the largest fjords in the world. Below, the water was studded with small islands and immense icebergs as intricately contoured as Inuit stone carvings. The sight brought out the fighter pilot in Epps. While Taylor hooted, he zoomed down fjords, the narrower the better, banking sharply until the plane's wings were vertical. Then he landed triumphantly in Narssarssuaq.

The adventure over, they left the same day for Goose Bay, Labrador, and from there returned to Atlanta. They'd only been gone a week, but the Far North — a frontier of snow and ice far from clients and contracts and stuffy jacket-and-tie affairs — had romanced them and they were smitten.

I N THE MONTHS TO COME, EPPS AND TAYLOR often relived their trip over drinks at the Downwind, an agreeable fliers' bar at DeKalb-Peachtree Airport in north Atlanta, where Epps Air Service was located. From time to time the talk turned to the Lost Squadron. Taylor was curious enough to call the Danish embassy in Washington, where an official confirmed that someone named Rajani in Atlanta had the salvage rights. Still, the Lost Squadron remained nothing more than an intriguing bit of aviation history until spring 1981, when a wealthy businessman taxied up to Epps's hangar in a brand-new Learjet.

"I swear, that's a beautiful airplane," Epps said.

"Yeah," the customer replied, "but I've always wanted a P-38."

Epps chuckled. "Well, sir, I know where six P-38s are."

Epps called Taylor that evening. "Hey, Richard, want to go north again?"

Contacting Rajani, he told him, "If you and Degan are still after those planes, we need to put a deal together. Got a customer for you."

It never took much to get Epps going. He didn't know a lot about vintage warbirds, but he'd learned that P-38s were rare — there were only a handful in flying condition in the world. If his wealthy customer wanted one, there was probably a market for them. If he and Taylor teamed up with Rajani and Degan, maybe they could bring the planes back from Greenland and somebody'd buy them. No matter what happened, it was an excellent excuse for an adventure in the north.

Soon, the Lost Squadron became the main topic of conversation whenever Epps and Taylor met at the Downwind. They imagined flying over the ice cap and spotting the planes just waiting to be found, their tails sticking above the snow.

Years later, Taylor would say, "We thought that all we'd have to do is shovel the snow off the wings, fill 'em with gas, crank 'em up and fly 'em off into the sunset. Guess we couldn't have been much more wrong."

PART ONE

THE LEGEND

CHAPTER ONE

SQUADRON DOWN

LIEUTENANT JOSEPH BRADLEY McMANUS shifted his position in the cramped cockpit of his P-38 fighter and glanced behind him at the faint outline of the Labrador coast. For a moment the boyish-looking twenty-four-year-old thought about his home in Philadelphia, his family, who were taking their summer holidays on a New Jersey beach, and his girlfriend, Elizabeth. But he knew sentimental reflections were potentially dangerous. Such thoughts threatened to rob a young pilot en route to a war in Europe of his nerve, a commodity McManus and his fellow airmen would soon be needing in surplus reserves. McManus looked down. What lay below was both exhilarating and sobering: dozens of weirdly shaped drifting icebergs floating in the cold, blue North Atlantic. As far as he could see, there wasn't anywhere to set down a P-38 and walk away afterward.

(Above) This photograph taken by pilot Brad McManus of the Lost Squadron shows planes of Tomcat Green over the Davis Strait. (Right) P-38s flying in formation. Nicknamed the "fork-tailed devil," the P-38 Lightning was one of the most celebrated Allied fighters of World War II.

Looking ahead, he was reassured to see *Big Stoop*, the massive B-17 "Flying Fortress" bomber that was his mother ship. McManus, a member of the 94th Fighter Squadron, First Fighter Group, was flying with Tomcat Green — four P-38s riding shotgun behind *Big Stoop* — which, along with the four P-38s and one B-17 of Tomcat Yellow, was part of Operation Bolero, a massive buildup of U.S. warplanes in Great Britain.

It was Tuesday, July 7, 1942, just seven months since the attack on Pearl Harbor had thrust the U.S. into the war. Although American forces were fighting the Japanese in the Pacific, President Franklin D. Roosevelt had declared a "Europe First" policy that gave priority to an invasion of Nazi-occupied France from English soil. In preparation for that eventual assault, American troops, tanks and planes were being shipped across the Atlantic. But the crossing was hazardous. Nazi U-boats were sinking Allied tankers and freighters at the rate of half a million tons each month, and much of the lost cargo consisted of aircraft.

The boldest aspect of Operation Bolero was a pioneering scheme to fly bombers and fighters overseas in stages, refueling at bases in Labrador, Greenland and Iceland.

The plan had been conceived by Major General Henry "Hap" Arnold, chief of the Army Air Force, who turned over responsibility for implementing the operation to Brigadier General Carl "Tooey" Spaatz, commander of the Eighth Air Force, which had been chosen to fight the air war from England. Of all the aircraft available to Spaatz, only the long-range B-17s and the newly designed twin-engine P-38s (outfitted with auxiliary drop-tanks) could manage the flight with any measure of safety. The four-engine B-17s were responsible for keeping the course and maintaining radio contact while the speedy high-altitude P-38s flanked the bombers, a pair on each wing.

Although the aircraft represented the most advanced technology available at the time, the talent didn't always match. To meet the need for pilots, the Army Air Force had lowered its entrance requirements for cadets and reduced flight training from twelve to seven months. As a result, the number of pilots receiving their wings increased from an annual average of three hundred in 1939 to thirty thousand by 1941. The most treacherous challenge facing these eager but inexperienced young "Roger Rudders" (as new pilots were called) was flying the North Atlantic ferry route.

Nonstop flights across the Atlantic began in 1919, but they were made by giant flying boats, floating airships or specially modified multiengine planes, not streamlined warplanes built for combat. In 1933,

The pilots and B-17 crew members of Tomcat Green and Tomcat Yellow pose at Labrador. Their flight was only the second of Operation Bolero's missions to ferry planes to Great Britain.

A snapshot of two Lightnings taken from a B-17 on the the Maine-to-Labrador leg of the trip.

Charles Lindbergh, fresh from his pioneering New York-to-Paris solo flight of 1927, made one of the earliest flights from the U.S. to England via Greenland and Iceland in a floatplane. Conditions tested the abilities of even the most experienced pilots. The unforgiving arctic weather could shift from clear skies to zero visibility and gale-force winds in minutes. Weather forecasting was primitive at best and, to make matters worse, radio transmission and reception were subject to unpredictable fade-outs over the northern latitudes, and proximity to the North Magnetic Pole sometimes made compasses spin erratically. To make it safely, the missions had to be flawlessly coordinated and the weather cooperative.

So far the flight had been uneventful. After receiving final instructions at Presque Isle, Maine, Tomcat Green and Tomcat Yellow had arrived at Goose Bay on July 4, where they'd remained for two days because of overcast. But the skies had been clear since the squadron departed Goose Bay two hours earlier. The planes were spread out in a loose formation that was easy for the pilots to maintain. McManus was flying in the outside position, well behind *Big Stoop*'s right wing, with Captain Robert B. Wilson, Tomcat Green's ranking officer and leader, ahead and slightly above him on his left. Flying behind the bomber's left wing were Lieutenant Carl Rudder and Lieutenant Harrison "Bugs" Lentz. About five miles ahead McManus could see Tomcat Yellow, made up of the second B-17, nicknamed *Do-Do*, with its P-38s in tow. Peering down, McManus saw a blanket of low-lying stratus clouds obscuring the ocean six thousand feet below. His radio crackled.

"Hello, Tomcat Yellow Leader. This is

Tomcat Yellow Commander calling. Request a position report."

McManus recognized the Texas drawl of Captain Dallas "Spider" Webb, the leader of Tomcat Yellow as well as the overall commander of the squadron. He was calling Lieutenant Jack Staples, *Do-Do*'s pilot. Through a blast of static came the reply.

"Twenty-five miles northwest of Point H, magnetic course 80 degrees, wind 25 miles per hour from 330 degrees, ground speed 195 miles per hour, reciprocal course 260 degrees. Over."

A few minutes later the planes flew into a heavy mass of cumulus clouds that reduced visibility to less than twenty-five feet. The "peashooters," as the bomber crews had dubbed the P-38s, closed into tight formation. Together, the planes rose in search of a break in the overcast. Emerging above the clouds at twenty-three thousand feet, they saw ahead another massive wall of white rising to thirty thousand feet and beyond. Turning north they tried to skirt the front as ice formed on the Plexiglas windshields of the P-38s.

What the hell is this all about? wondered McManus. In Goose Bay they'd been assured that the weather would be fine all the way to their destination, Bluie West One (BW-1), a secret base at Narssarssuaq near the southern tip of Greenland. Most of the P-38 pilots were wearing summer-weight flying suits and jackets. They hadn't anticipated flying at these altitudes, where temperatures dip well below freezing. McManus was beginning to lose the feeling in his fingers and toes.

Suddenly Staples radioed that he had a leak in his oxygen system and would have to descend to at least fifteen thousand feet. He took his B-17 down alone while the rest of the squadron circled overhead, waiting for him to report on conditions. Finally they heard his voice.

"Hello, Yellow Commander, this is Yellow Leader calling. I'm at ten thousand and it's pretty broken down here. I think you can make it without much trouble."

McManus watched as the four Tomcat Yellow peashooters spiraled down through a hole in the clouds to join their leader. Then *Big Stoop*'s pilot, Lieutenant Joe Hanna, dropped his nose into the soup at two hundred miles per hour. For the peppy P-38s, flying blindly through dense gray fog in tight formation behind the lumbering B-17 was like asking supercharged racing cars to keep pace behind a family sedan. McManus's eyes narrowed in concentration and his heart knocked like a broken piston. Every muscle in his body tightened as he jockeyed the throttle, struggling to edge his plane closer to the B-17, his wingtip nearly touching Wilson's beside him. If a pilot fell even a dozen feet behind, he might lose sight of the others and become lost.

Tomcat Green dropped to ten thousand feet, then to five thousand, to three thousand and finally to two thousand, searching in vain for clear sky. From some distance away, the Tomcat Yellow pilots could be faintly heard over the radio, but it was too dangerous to try to re-form the squadron in the clouds. The two elements were on their own. It was past the halfway point of the flight, so a decision would have to be made whether to continue toward BW-1, divert to Bluie West 8 (an alternate base five hundred miles north of BW-1) or return to Goose Bay. As Staples and his navigator tried to figure out which base was closest, Spider Webb burst in, "Hello, Yellow Leader. I don't give a damn what you do, but do it quick!"

When Hanna asked for a fuel report, it became clear that the P-38s were running dangerously low. *Big Stoop*'s radio operator was getting nothing but static. According to Hanna's calculations, if they flew slowly at low altitude to conserve fuel, they could just make it to Goose Bay.

As the element leader, R. B. Wilson gave the order and Tomcat Green banked sharply 180 degrees, heading back to Labrador. An hour later the planes emerged out of the overcast and found themselves over the iceberg-studded North Atlantic. Still, *Big Stoop*'s navigator was unsure of their exact position. As the needles on his fuel gauges sank, McManus imagined bailing out into the frigid water or, when he caught sight of land on the distant horizon, onto the bleak Labrador coastline while his pilotless P-38 hurtled toward destruction. Expecting to see Goose Bay at any moment, the exasperated fighter pilots were instead informed that the young B-17 navigators had miscalculated by several hundred miles. The radio crackled with the wisecracks of worried men.

"Get those emergency boats ready, Hanna."

"If I get back, I'll drink a whole quart of whiskey in one gulp."

"You can say that again, brother."

As the planes finally approached Goose Bay, Hanna radioed a warning to the tower. "All little Tomcats of Green flight almost out of gas. Clear the field."

McManus felt like an old man when he clambered out of the cockpit, and he could see that the others looked no better. He was tired, cold and hungry. His muscles ached from sitting in the same position for eight hours and from the tension of flying through bad weather and only just making it back on the vapors in his gas tanks. He attributed being alive to a heavenly measure of luck. Luck had been with Tomcat Yellow as well; the planes had landed safely at BW-8.

Privately everyone felt relief, although some of the P-38 pilots had sharp words for weather forecasters and B-17 navigators. Being cocky young fighter pilots, though, everybody laughed off their brush with disaster.

"Just a little bad weather."

(continued on page 31)

Members of Tomcat Green killing time at Goose Bay. After the weather made it impossible to reach the base in Greenland, their flight turned back for Labrador.

The Fork-tailed Devil

ONE OF THE MOST ADVANCED AND VERSATILE combat planes of World War II, Lockheed's P-38 Lightning was the fastest, most heavily armed fighter in the skies. It served as a medium-altitude fighter-bomber, high-altitude precision bomber, bomber escort, torpedo plane, radar-equipped night fighter and long-range observation and photo-reconnaissance plane. While the twin-engine Lightning was a powerful weapon against the Axis powers in the European and Mediterranean theaters, it was indispensable in the Pacific, where its range (extended by auxiliary fuel tanks) permitted it to fly dangerous missions over vast distances and return safely to base. It lacked the maneuverability of its premier adversaries — Germany's Messerschmitt 109 and Japan's Mitsubishi Zero — but the P-38 frequently triumphed because of its speed (greater than 400 miles per hour), awesome firepower (20-mm nose cannon supplemented by four .50-caliber machine guns) and rugged, heavily armored construction. The Japanese described it as "two airplanes with one pilot" and the Germans dubbed it *der gabelschwanz teufel* — "the fork-tailed devil."

In 1937, with the threat of Hitler's Germany gradually persuading U.S. politicians to change their isolationist policies, the Army Air Corps

(Right) The P-38F model was the version of the successful Lightning fighter flown by the Lost Squadron.

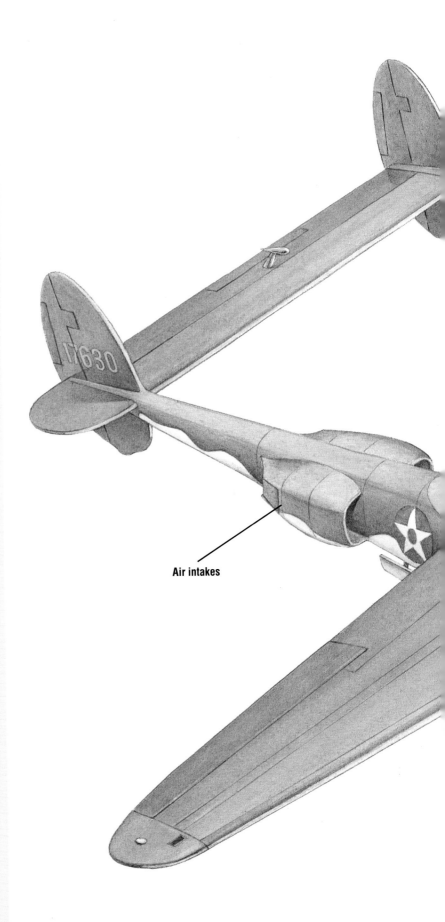

Air intakes

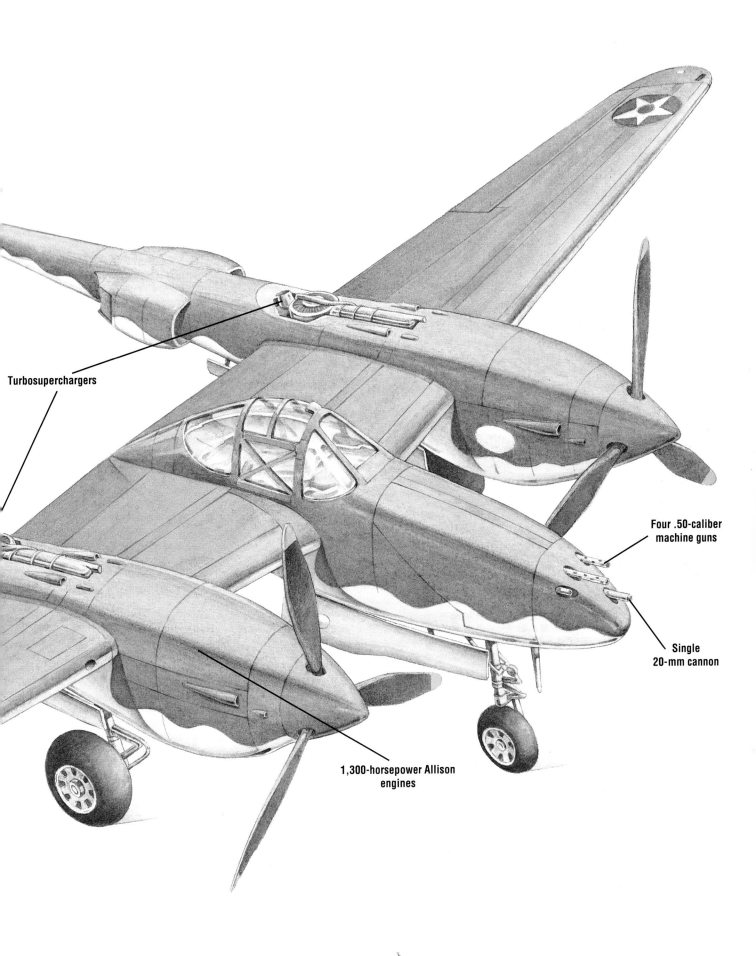

Turbosuperchargers

Four .50-caliber
machine guns

Single
20-mm cannon

1,300-horsepower Allison
engines

circulated "Specification X-608" to aircraft manufacturers. It called for a long-range pursuit and escort fighter able to reach altitudes and speeds far beyond any plane then in production. Working out of Lockheed's development facility in Burbank, which later became the legendary "Skunk Works", engineers Clarence "Kelly" Johnson and Hall Hibbard came up with a rad-

ical prototype, the XP-38, which won the company its first military contract.

At 15,000 pounds, the XP-38 was 150 per cent larger than conventional single-engine combat planes. Its size and twin-boom design made it look more like a small bomber than a fighter. In an aviation industry still dominated by fabric-covered frames, it featured metal surfaces that were assembled using the latest in aeronautical construction techniques. At a time when air-cooled engines were the norm, a pair of powerful and efficient liquid-cooled Allison V-12s were mounted on the wings, boosted by newly designed General Motors turbosuperchargers located in the booms. It was the first aircraft of any kind to use a fully retractable tricycle landing gear, and the five guns mounted in the nose provided accurate and devastating firepower. Admiring onlookers often compared the streamlined fighter to a sleek European racing car.

Despite a crash landing on its maiden flight, the XP-38 impressed Army Air Corps officials enough to order thirteen more planes, the first

(Above) Clarence "Kelly" Johnson, a Lockheed designer, created a series of preliminary sketches (right) for a long-range, twin-engine fighter that eventually evolved into the P-38 Lightning (below).

(Opposite) A P-38 Lightning shows off its distinctive twin-boom tail to advantage. (Opposite below) From the prototype built by Lockheed, the XP-38, through to mass production, the Lightning changed very little.

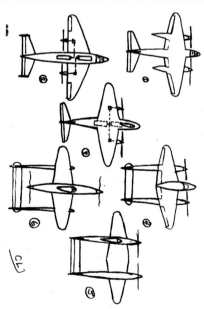

27

(Above) Designed as fighters, Lightnings were used in many other roles. Attempts were even made to use it as a torpedo bomber, although no torpedo-equipped Lightnings ever saw combat.

of nearly ten thousand (in eighteen versions) that would be built before the end of the war. At first, Lockheed christened the plane Atlanta, but Britain's Royal Air Force, which received the first shipment of P-38s, renamed it Lightning. It was not surprising that Lockheed quickly adopted the more colorful British appellation. The P-38 was so fast that during high-speed dives the plane shook uncontrollably, and many pilots crashed before Lockheed's engineers were able to make design modifications. Later, engineers realized that the P-38 was the first plane to travel at near supersonic speeds, where it experienced aerodynamic conditions that were poorly understood in the 1940s.

In the Pacific, the P-38 was the preeminent fighter. With its twin engines and extra fuel tanks, it was the only plane that could manage long-distance missions across vast stretches of ocean, and many badly damaged P-38s made it safely back to base on one engine. The two top-scoring USAF aces of all time — Majors Richard Bong and Thomas McGuire — flew P-38s in the Pacific, as did Colonel Charles MacDonald, the third-highest

scoring P-38 ace, who ranks fifth overall.

P-38s were involved in what is regarded as one of the most significant missions in the Pacific. After U.S. cryptographers broke the Japanese navy's secret code in spring 1943, they learned the travel itinerary for Admiral Isoruku Yamamoto, a brilliant strategist and architect of Japan's attack on Pearl Harbor. Sixteen P-38s made the 1,000-mile round trip from Guadalcanal to Bougainville in the Solomon Islands. In a perfectly timed aerial ambush, two Mitsubishi Betty bombers — one of which contained Yamamoto — and five Zeros were shot down. (Controversy continues to this day over which attacking pilot deserves credit for destroying Yamamoto's plane.)

Despite its distinguished record, few P-38s survived the end of the war. At a time when the first jets were coming into service, the U.S. military designated the P-51 Mustang as its main propeller-driven fighter. Many Lightnings were broken up overseas rather than being transported back to the U.S. for disposal. Today, the P-38 Lightning is a rare species of warbird. By the 1980s, only half a dozen in flying condition remained.

(Left) As well as performing different roles, Lightnings served in every theater of war, from the Pacific to northern Europe and Iceland.

(Above) The Pacific was where the Lightning really came into its own. The large distances between islands and from base to base made the long-range twin-engined fighter perfect for the region. Many of America's top aces made their mark there flying the Lightning. Among them were (left) all-time highest-scoring American ace Richard Bong, shown here on a goodwill tour of the U.S., and (below) Charles MacDonald (on right), fifth-highest-scoring ace in the USAAF, standing here in front of his P-38, Putt-Putt Maru.

(Left) The aircrew quarters at Goose Bay. (Below left) The airstrip at BW-1 ran alongside a mountain-ringed fjord. (Below) Bad weather kept Tomcat Green at BW-1 for two days.

To reach BW-8, where Tomcat Yellow was waiting, Tomcat Green flew north over Greenland's coastal mountains.

BW-8 was also located on the coast, several hundred miles north of BW-1.

"Maybe Hitler invented himself a cloud-making machine."

It had been a close call, McManus thought, but surely a fluke. The Army Air Force wouldn't be sending its hot new P-38s island-hopping across the Atlantic if it didn't know they'd make it. Next time the weather reports would be accurate.

ON SUNDAY, JULY 12, McMANUS AND THE rest of Tomcat Green flew uneventfully to BW-1. A newly built air base nestled between 5,000-foot mountains at the end of a jagged fjord, BW-1 was the center of American military operations in Greenland. They waited there for two days until a storm front passed, then on Tuesday, July 14, flew north to BW-8 to rejoin Tomcat Yellow. After checking in at operations, the men climbed aboard a truck that took them to the camp and mess hall. They enjoyed their first showers since leaving the U.S. ten days earlier and shopped for cigarettes and candy at the commissary. Then they turned in for what they thought would be a good night's rest.

At midnight, after only a few hours' sleep, they were awakened and told to prepare for takeoff. The sun never sets during Greenland summers, and the sky was pearl gray at 3:00 A.M. as the Lightnings warmed up, their 1,300-horsepower Allisons roaring at an earsplitting pitch, the turbosuperchargers glowing cherry red and long snakes of blue flame shooting out the exhausts. At ten thousand feet, as the planes circled and fell into formation, the sun glowed scarlet over the mountains, glinting dully off their metal skins.

Greenland's mountains extend the entire length of both coasts, enclosing a vast two-mile-thick ice cap that occupies nearly 700,000 square miles — 82 per cent of the island. At the edges of the cap, the ice flows through mountain valleys, creating dramatic glaciers that work their way slowly to the coast where colossal icebergs break off and float out to sea. (In 1912 the ocean liner *Titanic* struck one of these icebergs and sank, taking two-thirds of her 2,200 passengers with her.) The next leg of the trip would take the squadron southeast over the ice cap and the mountains of the east coast, then across the Denmark Strait to Reykjavik, Iceland.

There were now only six P-38s — both Bugs Lentz and Bucky Starbuck, one of the Tomcat Yellow pilots, had suffered mechanical problems and been forced to stay behind. As the squadron soared across the ice cap at twelve thousand feet, a heavy overcast began to form. They rose above it, and the temperature dropped to minus ten degrees Fahrenheit. Then, ninety minutes from Iceland, the planes hit a mass of cumulus clouds, which forced them up another two thousand feet. McManus's feet were so cold he could barely feel the rudder pedals. *Hope this isn't going to be a repeat of last week's trip*, he thought. He tried to warm himself up by visualizing his parents sitting in bathing suits on a sandy beach. In the Lightning next to McManus's, R. B. Wilson had impulsively torn the defroster from its mounting. He was using it to heat his gloves in an effort to keep his hands warm enough to feel the controls. Spotting an opening in the clouds, Wilson informed

By early morning on July 15, Tomcat Green and Tomcat Yellow were airborne again, on their way to Iceland.

From BW-8 the reunited flights headed east over Greenland's ice cap. Brad McManus snapped this shot from his P-38, showing Greenland's mountains poking above the heavy overcast blanketing the surface.

Big Stoop's wings, their props no more than a few inches from the big ship's flaps. Ice crystals flowing over the B-17's wings like a baby snowstorm often left the P-38 pilots in whiteout conditions. Wilson ordered Hanna to climb out of the mess, and the bomber began to rise at approximately 120 miles per hour.

The P-38s, never comfortable at low speeds, were struggling. McManus looked in horror at the ice building up on his wings, making the controls sluggish in his hands. The Lightning's engines growled under the weight of the ice, and the turbo-superchargers cut in and out, forcing him to nudge the throttle continually just to keep up, burning precious fuel. Many of the fighters nearly stalled (reached the point at which a plane's speed is too low to maintain its forward momentum) and fell back in the sky.

At sixteen thousand feet, the planes broke through the overcast and rejoined Tomcat Yellow. Everyone was relieved, although it was hard to say which was worse — flying through the storm or watching your skin turn blue at the higher altitudes. They were now only an hour from Reykjavik, but another massive front lay ahead. Over the radio someone plotted revenge against weather forecasters.

After flying south for fifteen minutes trying to find a way around the front, Hanna reported that his radio operator was unable to raise either Reykjavik or a weather plane that was supposed to be flying about an hour ahead. Then Staples, piloting *Do-Do*, the lead B-17, announced that his airspeed indicator had frozen. Without

Spider Webb that he was taking Tomcat Green down to look for clear weather beneath the overcast.

They descended into pitch-blackness and a hellish arctic storm. As the hole above them closed, the clouds became as dense and heavy as cotton wool drenched in tar. Rain and snow squalls reduced visibility to less than a plane's length. McManus could see the blurred outlines of Wilson and Rudder tucked behind the trailing edge of that vital instrument, he couldn't lead through overcast, so Hanna's *Big Stoop* took over. Finally, at 7:15 A.M., Spider Webb's voice was heard over the radio.

"Set a course for home. We're going back."

The squadron turned one-eighty and headed northwest toward BW-8. An hour later, through a gap in the clouds, they glimpsed the rocky east coast of Greenland and the ice cap stretching beyond it. But what had been a broken layer of stratus earlier in the morning had developed into a solid blanket of scudding clouds rising in layers. When they tried to plow through a bank of the stuff at twelve thousand feet, conditions proved to be as bad as they'd been the previous week. Meanwhile the B-17 radio operators tried fruitlessly to contact BW-8 while the navigators struggled to establish accurate position reports — virtually impossible with an overcast obscuring the sun and clouds below concealing landmarks. They were flying by dead reckoning in unfamiliar surroundings. By this time the P-38s had dropped their auxiliary gas tanks. Everyone had enough fuel to reach BW-8, but not to fool around much on the way. Over the radio Lieutenant Harry Smith, piloting one of Tomcat Yellow's Lightnings, made a grim joke: "Wouldn't it be too bad if BW-8's closed?"

About 130 miles from the base, the B-17s received a coded message, apparently from BW-8, which the pilots relayed to their fighter escorts. "Ceiling twelve hundred feet. Visibility one-eighth of a mile." McManus was shocked. If that report was correct, it would be suicide to attempt to pick their

way between the rocky peaks that formed the narrow corridor leading to BW-8's runway. He heard Webb order a verification of the report, this time "in the clear," or uncoded. A message came back, again in code, confirming that BW-8 was socked in.

Spotting a hole in the clouds, McManus and several other P-38 pilots decided to take a look at the ice cap, just in case they had to make an emergency landing. As he hurtled along at an altitude of one hundred feet, McManus surveyed the topography. It was hard to estimate your height above the glistening white surface, and a low-lying ghostly haze blended against the ice, effectively whiting out the horizon. Any attempt to land would have to be carefully planned and executed. Still, he'd heard that less than three weeks earlier a B-17 had successfully made a forced landing on the ice cap not far from BW-8.

By the time they'd rejoined the squadron between cloud layers, the B-17s had received a message from BW-1 that its runway was open. Deep inside the chalky overcast, the navigators plotted a new course. It was 10:00 A.M. Estimated time of arrival at BW-1: noon.

McManus checked his fuel gauges. Then he radioed R. B. Wilson. "Hope they're right," he said, "because if they're wrong by as much as five minutes I won't make it."

(When officials later compared Allied weather records to the coded messages received by the pilots, they discovered that the reported weather conditions at BW-8 and BW-1 had been switched. Although it was never proved, they speculated that the false information may have been sent by either a U-boat or a secret Nazi radio station located somewhere on the east coast.)

Flying at less than 150 miles per hour to conserve fuel, the planes picked their way between heavy layers of cloud. Occasionally a shaft of sunlight broke through, but otherwise the clouds were so dense that they appeared to envelop the entire ice cap. After ninety minutes, to the pilots' immense relief, they spotted the towering coastal mountains through an opening in the cloud cover. But where on the west coast were they in relation to BW-1?

Banking toward the open sky, the pilots checked their compasses and calculated the deviation. At about the same moment, everyone realized that something was very wrong. The ice cap crept nearly to the water's edge, which only occurred at two places on the west coast, and they shouldn't have been near either of them. Furthermore, the position of the mountains and ocean seemed to be reversed, like a mirror image. It was a funhouse mirror: they were

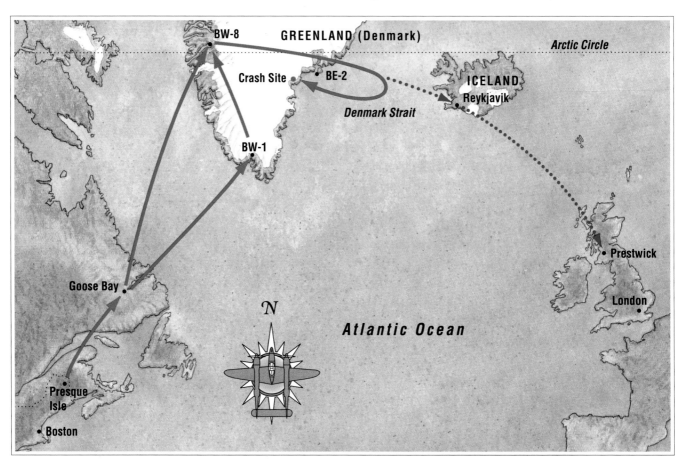

The original plan called for Tomcat Green and Tomcat Yellow to fly to BW-1 in Greenland, then to Iceland and finally to Scotland. Bad weather forced Tomcat Yellow north to BW-8, and Tomcat Green back to Goose Bay. Tomcat Green then flew to BW-1 and joined up with Tomcat Yellow at BW-8. While crossing the Denmark Strait, they were forced back to Greenland.

back on the east coast of Greenland.

McManus's heart sank. The numbers weren't in his favor. They were still two hours away from BW-1, and his remaining twenty-four gallons of fuel would last about twenty minutes. While the others circled and the radio buzzed with anxious conversation, he thought, *We're kidding ourselves. We're miles from anyplace. I'm going down.*

When McManus announced his decision, it prompted a discussion among his fellow pilots about whether to try it with the landing gear down, or up for a belly landing. Carl Rudder, who had completed two forced landings with wheels up during training, said that the reinforced steel underside of the P-38 could withstand considerable impact. The rule of thumb, Rudder warned McManus, was to keep the gear up anytime you didn't know for sure what the surface was like.

At 11:40 A.M. McManus broke away from the squadron and descended toward the ice cap. R. B. Wilson, Tomcat Green's leader, followed him down and pulled alongside, while Lieutenant Robert H. "Egghead" Wilson (no relation), a Tomcat Yellow pilot who was a close friend of McManus's, flew behind.

While the rest of the squadron circled overhead, McManus skimmed very low over the ice cap, trying to determine the direction of the wind. (Landing into the wind would help him slow down more quickly.) The weather had cleared considerably except for a high overcast, and the surface looked promising: icy and hard-packed, flat as a billiard table. Despite Rudder's warning, McManus badly wanted to make a conventional landing. During briefings at Goose

Bay, they'd been told that no one had ever attempted a wheels-down landing on the ice cap, but they were also told that it might be possible. McManus knew that if he were successful and rescuers later dropped fuel supplies, he could gas up and take off again, salvaging a brand-new fighter.

He flipped the microphone switch on the control yoke.

"So long, fellas," he said, trying to sound jaunty. "See you later."

Feeling his way down cautiously, McManus dropped his flaps and lowered his landing gear. At 110 miles per hour he gently touched the surface, nudged the throttle to lift off again, then dropped down again and rolled a little farther, testing the terrain. It felt solid. He touched down at 70 miles per hour, his nose high, his rear wheels rolling along the ice. For a couple of hundred yards it appeared to be a textbook landing. The plane had slowed to 60 miles per hour by the time the nose wheel touched down. It broke through the ice, the landing gear buckled and, in a single, sickening motion, eight tons of aircraft flipped heavily onto its back.

Had it struck tarmac, concrete, gravel or even hard-packed soil, the P-38's bubble canopy would have been crushed, and McManus with it. Fortunately a glaze of ice over a few feet of snow is a more forgiving surface. *You stupid idiot* was the first thought that came into McManus's mind; then, after collecting his wits, he began to evaluate his predicament. On the minus side, he had crashed his plane and was hanging upside down from his safety belt and parachute stays in absolute blackness inside what was left of his cockpit, now buried in snow and beginning to fill with smoke. On the plus side, he was alive. Outside, he could hear the roar of P-38s buzzing over the wreckage.

Fire was always a danger after a plane crash, but the smoke dissipated almost as soon as it appeared. McManus figured he wasn't carrying enough fuel to face a serious threat, but he didn't intend to stay in the cockpit long enough to find out. Struggling to remain calm, he switched off the circuits and unfastened his safety belt. Locating his army knife, he cut himself free of his parachute and rolled down the cockpit's side window. Then he twisted himself into position, shoved his legs through the narrow opening and began kicking his way out.

FROM THE AIR, R. H. WILSON watched as his friend upended his ship in a cloud of snow. A puff of smoke rose in the air. There was no sign of anyone crawling from under the wreckage.

Wilson turned around and brought his plane in for a landing. He lowered his flaps but prudently kept his landing gear up. Seconds before he touched down, as his props were skimming the ice, he flipped off the master switch to reduce the risk of fire. Less than a minute later he slid to a smooth stop.

Grabbing the first-aid kit, Wilson leaped out of his cockpit. He could see McManus's plane about half a mile away, but with every step his flying boots sank nearly a foot into the soft snow, and he was exhausted by the time he reached it. What had appeared to be smoke from the beginnings of a fire turned out to be steam rising from the radiators. Furthermore, a dazed McManus clambered from under a wing and staggered to his feet just as Wilson reached him.

"Well, Egghead, didn't think I'd make it, did you?" McManus said. Then he turned and waved to the pilots flying overhead, who responded by doing slow rolls and other acrobatics.

Wilson, noticing that something had sliced right through McManus's heavy winter flying jacket, discovered a two-inch gash on his arm. "Better take care of that," Wilson said, ripping open a packet of sulfanilamide, the antibacterial wonder

Brad McManus and pal pose beside his flipped P-38.

A P-38 on the ice cap. The plane's propellers and hubs have broken off on contact with the ice and been left behind in its trail.

drug of the day. He sprinkled a little on McManus's wound and covered it with a compress bandage.

One by one the remaining pilots came in for successful wheels-up landings. Harry Smith was the last to land, bringing in his Lightning so smoothly he didn't even bend the props. Even though he was in the middle of nowhere, Smith dutifully filled out his checklist before joining the others at McManus's plane.

Photos, taken with a bellows-style Kodak camera that McManus's father had given him, show grinning young men striking self-consciously casual poses in front of the flipped P-38. They sport the same insouciant expressions that young racing-car drivers wear after emerging uninjured from a high-speed crash.

The B-17s, with their greater fuel capacity, remained aloft for half an hour, sending SOS signals without receiving a reply. The navigators calculated their position as 65° 20' north latitude, 40° 20' west longitude — near the east coast, less than a hundred miles from the spot they'd crossed three hours earlier after turning back from Iceland. They'd flown in a huge semicircle over the ice cap. It was not a proud moment for the navigators. Finally, the B-17s skimmed smoothly along the ice, smashing the ball turrets located on the underside of the planes and bending their props, but otherwise landing undamaged.

Do-Do on the ice cap. The ship's number four engine is running.

Big Stoop at rest on the ice cap.

chocolate. (In anticipation of rationing in war-torn England, some of the officers had their own stashes containing items such as whiskey, ham and chocolate, in addition to silk stockings and lipstick.)

Warnings were issued not to eat excessive amounts of snow (to prevent sore throats) and to wear sunglasses at all times (to prevent snow blindness). Crews transformed the insides of the bombers — renamed Hotel *Do-Do* and Hotel *Big Stoop* — into something approximating sleeping quarters for two dozen men. Despite his protests, McManus was given a canteen cup of 90-proof medicine and tucked away in a sleeping bag inside *Big Stoop*, where he slept for nearly twenty-four hours. Meanwhile, aerials suspended from box kites were flown above the crash site while the radio operators sent continuous SOS signals. With all the magnetic interference and weather turbulence in the area, however, it was not clear whether they were getting through.

Lieutenant Jack Staples listens in on a B-17's radio. From the moment they landed, the big bombers' radio operators tried to make contact with the outside.

Concerned about exhausting their planes' batteries, the crews examined the engines of their B-17s to see whether they could be run. Luckily they were undamaged. A shallow trench was dug beneath *Big Stoop*'s number one engine so the propeller blades would clear the snow, while several men hacksawed two feet off the blades of one of *Do-Do*'s

After they had crash-landed, the stranded aviators converted the B-17s into living quarters for their crews and the Lightning pilots.

On the ice, the stranded airmen quickly began turning their downed ships into a survival camp. Squadron leader Dallas Webb took command. The B-17 crews were to shelter inside their ships, and the P-38 pilots would move into the B-17s they had flown behind. As ranking officers, Webb took command of *Do-Do* and R. B. Wilson of *Big Stoop*. Although they were confident that they would be rescued, rations were pooled and divided to last two weeks, limiting each man to one proper meal per day, plus a candy bar and a cup of hot props. With both engines running, the batteries were kept charged. Unhappily, efforts to devise a system to heat the bombers failed, and the men spent a cold night, dressed in their fleece-lined leather flying suits and whatever spare clothing they had, buried in sleeping bags.

The next day, Thursday, July 16, was cold. A fog enveloped the ice cap, accompanied by rain and a chilling wind, which everyone knew would ground any potential search parties. While the radio operators repeatedly sent position reports, others used their ingenuity to improve on their first day's crude efforts at building a camp. A helmet filled with a mixture of gasoline and oil served as a rudimentary cookstove. A member of one of the bomber crews figured out how to heat the B-17s. He took a metal oxygen bottle and cut a hole in either end with a hacksaw. An engine exhaust manifold pipe was wired tightly over one hole and run like a flue through the fuselage wall. A tin can lid served as a damper over the other hole. Then oil drained from the engines and turbosuperchargers was dripped into the canister using a parachute strap for a wick. Each of the B-17s had one of the contraptions mounted against the inside wall of the fuselage, where it served as a space heater.

The third day, Friday, was clear and sunny, but there was still no response to the radio signals, and some of the men were growing pessimistic. They passed the time by sleeping or playing gin rummy or hearts. Finally one of the radio operators received a message in Morse code asking about injuries and supplies that were needed and

confirming their position. As word spread through the camp the reaction was electric. Men whooped and hollered, leaping in the air and dancing in the snow.

Later that day two C-47 transport planes were spotted in the distance. The excited men shot off flares and waved until the planes made a low, slow pass. Anticipating a supply drop, the men ignited a smoke pot to help the pilots judge the wind, which was gusting as high as fifty miles per hour. A package was dropped by parachute, but as soon as it reached the ground the wind picked it up and sent it hurtling across the ice cap until it disappeared. Fanning out as the planes made additional drops, the men managed to snag and smother the parachutes. Inside burlap bags were blankets, sleeping bags, food, whiskey, medical supplies and — a little pilots' humor — condoms. As the planes soared away, they blinked the message "Goodbye and good luck."

One of the stranded fliers prepares a meal over a makeshift cookstove in the lee of a B-17.

Brad McManus lounges on the wing of his P-38.

Lieutenant Jack Staples (right) and his crew from

P-38 pilot R. B. Wilson.

Lieutenant R. H. Wilson sits on his engine hub.

From that time on, knowing that rescue was imminent, everyone relaxed. R. B. Wilson removed the battery-powered radio beam receiver from his P-38 and was able to pick up news reports and music from Iceland and England. One day the men held an impromptu square dance on the wing of *Big Stoop*. Draping a torn parachute over his shoulders like a cape, Carl Rudder performed an exotic dance before an audience of pilots and bomber crew. During high winds, some of the men stood on burlap bags and held small parachutes aloft until they hurtled across the ice cap, a kind of makeshift ice-surfing.

On Saturday, July 18, the unmistakable shape of a navy Catalina flying boat came into view. Its pilot, Lieutenant George Atterbury, would become a welcome and regular presence over the ice cap in the days to come. Aside from dropping numerous packages filled with sleeping bags and blankets, canned foods, whiskey and magazines, Atterbury relayed messages from BW-1 and BW-8 and kept the stranded men up to date on the progress of a rescue party from a small coastal weather station one hundred miles to the north.

In his Catalina flying boat Lieutenant George Atterbury became a frequent visitor to the stranded airmen, dropping supplies and radioing them updates on the rescue party headed their way.

Preparing a meal on a makeshift cookstove.

Carl Rudder entertains the troops with a parachute striptease.

(Above) Downed fliers, with little to do but wait, lounge on Do-Do. (Right) Others used parachutes and sacking for joy rides.

ON THE MORNING OF JULY 16, SERGEANT Oran Earl Toole, a twenty-year-old radio operator, received a coded message that a plane had been forced down on the ice cap. Toole was assigned to Bluie East 2 (BE-2), located near the Danish settlement of Angmagssalik on Greenland's east coast. BE-2 was a radio and meteorological station designed to provide accurate weather information and on-course signals to pilots flying the hazardous northern route to England. In reality it was, like most American military operations just seven months into the war, an example of good intentions held together by hardworking but largely inexperienced enlisted men. Toole, who was fifteen months out of radio operators' school, had just managed to get the navigational beacon on the air and was beginning to test it. There were no aircraft, Coast Guard icebreakers or trained rescue personnel based at BE-2, so Toole couldn't imagine that a downed plane would have any impact on his duties.

By the time a few more messages arrived, though, the place was buzzing. It wasn't one plane that had crash-landed on the ice cap, but eight, and one pilot who flipped his plane was reportedly injured. It was a bona fide catastrophe, but BW-8's commanding officer, the famous rescue specialist Bernt Balchen, was involved in another rescue mission at the time. Instead Toole's commanding officer, Lieutenant Fred Crockett, who had been with Admiral Richard Byrd's expedition to Antarctica in 1929 and had many years of arctic experience, was given the responsibility of rescuing the downed fliers.

Crockett assembled a rescue crew of Toole; Donald Shaw, a trained sled-dog driver; mechanic Robert Beale; and Donald Kent, whose trips to the north with his father, the renowned American painter

Sergeant Oran Earl Toole was the radio operator at BE-2 when the word came in that eight planes had ditched on the ice.

Lieutenant Fred Crockett was in charge of the hastily organized rescue party that left BE-2 to reach the downed airmen.

Members of the rescue party with their boat, the thirty-foot Uma Tauva.

Rockwell Kent, had earned him a posting as an "arctic adviser." Had any of the marooned airmen on the ice cap seen the rescue party as it departed BE-2 on the morning of Friday, July 17, their optimism might have been tempered.

The men wore a mixture of uniforms and foul-weather gear, some of it of their own design. It gave them the appearance of belonging to a military organization, although of what branch or country was hard to say. Their rescue vessel, the *Uma Tauva*, was a thirty-foot open wooden launch of the Chesapeake clam-digger type that rode low in the water and was under-powered by a four-cycle inboard marine engine. Toole had recently outfitted the launch with makeshift radio equipment, but it wasn't a lot better than the ham-radio setup he'd operated from his parents' home. Behind their launch they pulled an old white dory, rented from the Danish governor of Angmagssalik, that carried a homemade sled, trail gear and five yowling sled dogs.

The rescue party moved slowly down the coast, picking its way around the menacing pack ice. The ice, ranging from patio-sized slabs to arena-sized sheets, could crush a small boat in an instant. At one point, the launch was jammed between an impassable mass of ice and an iceberg the size of a bungalow. Toole, navigating from the bow, directed the launch at full speed toward a hole in the center of the iceberg. The opening looked just deep enough to sail through, and for a heart-stopping few moments the men waited for the sickening crunch that would signal their transition from rescue party to shipwreck victims. Instead the launch shot smoothly through the hole and emerged into open water on the other side.

Four days later, on Tuesday, July 21, after many attempts to find a lead through the ice, the *Uma Tauva* landed on the rocky shore-line. A steep cliff rose several hundred feet to the edge of the ice cap, where slow-moving ice poured through gorges on its way to the sea. Before long Toole heard the drone of a plane's engines and set off distress flares. Soon Atterbury circled overhead. Unable to find Atterbury's navy frequency, Toole could receive but not transmit, so Atterbury

Among the equipment they took was a sled and five dogs to pull it, meant to carry out the pilot who had been reported injured.

ingeniously asked questions that could be answered yes or no, to which Toole signaled his replies with a bolt of bright yellow cloth.

The next day the dogs were hitched to the sled and Crockett, Shaw and Kent, all expert skiers, began the trip inland, carefully marking their trail for the return trip. Although it was only ten miles to the planes, zigzagging around crevasses turned it into a seventeen-mile trek. Atterbury flew back and forth along the route, radioing the downed fliers that help was on the way and shepherding Crockett's team around dangerous crevasses. In the meantime the Coast Guard cutter *Northland* had reached BE-2 and would soon be on its way.

At the crash site preparations for departure began. The P-38 pilots returned to their ships to retrieve personal effects. Some fired .45 slugs into precious electronic equipment in case Nazi scavengers

descended on the site. McManus sadly visited his plane for the last time and removed the clock from its instrument panel as a keepsake.

"There they are," shouted a lookout posted atop *Big Stoop*. A mob of exuberant fliers rushed to greet the rescue party.

"There's only one sled!" exclaimed Harry Smith, grinning. "How are the rest of you guys going to get out?"

In fact, none of the men had anticipated a seventeen-mile hike. McManus had envisioned a battalion of sleds, one to a man. (Decades later he would learn the sled had been intended for him, the pilot thought to have been injured when his plane flipped. When Crockett discovered McManus was fine, he used the sled to carry sensitive equipment salvaged from the B-17s.)

They left late in the evening, when the sun was at its lowest point in the sky and

With rescue near, the airmen prepare to leave the site.

R. B. Wilson assembles his gear, as others behind him scramble to get ready.

Carl Rudder packs his bag.

The moment of arrival of the rescue party as photographed by Brad McManus.

The sled had been brought for Brad McManus, on the belief that he was too badly hurt to walk.

the cooler air had created a crust on the snow that made walking easier. Nonetheless, the men sank midway to their knees with each step. Despite Crockett's warning to bring as little as possible, backpacks were filled to capacity and many men hauled toboggans made out of P-38 canopies and engine cowlings attached to ropes or parachute harnesses. At one point Harry Smith looked back to see R. B. Wilson and Joe Hanna pulling a two-man version that was so overloaded it looked as though they were dragging a B-17 engine.

Crockett led the way on skis, stopping every half hour for a few minutes of rest. McManus and Carl Rudder were not far behind, having elected to travel light. They wore their flight jackets, trousers and boots, and McManus carried only a small pack containing his camera and flight manual. As they trudged toward the coast, McManus looked back to see the rest of the squadron forming a straggling line a mile long. Somewhere near the back, Wilson and Hanna strained like workhorses to haul their sled. Wilson's mother had given him green ski pajamas, which for sentimental reasons he refused to part with and had pulled on over

his uniform, earning him the nickname Green Hornet.

As McManus and Rudder reached the top of each hill they expected to see the coast, but there was always another hill. As the hours passed and a morning sun warmed the ice cap, the men stripped off layers of clothing, only to have to pull them on again whenever they rested in the cold wind. Soon the trail was littered with discarded clothing and gear: trench coats, uniforms, blankets, food, handguns, even a pair of roller skates. Wilson and Hanna finally abandoned their sled and reduced their load to a shoulder bag each. From time to time a man would collapse in the snow, then, drawing on an unknown cache of energy, haul himself to his feet and continue. From the air it looked like an itinerant gypsy circus that was self-destructing.

"How much further?"

"How much longer?"

"This is God-awful."

"I don't think I'm going to make it."

McManus was among the first to reach the base camp and stagger to the edge of the ice cap. Below him was a steep cliff face leading to the ocean. A small boat was moored there.

(Left) The rocky beach below the ice cap. Uma Tauva is moored offshore. (Right) Uma Tauva makes her way through the ice to the cutter Northland.

Once everyone had arrived and had some field rations and coffee, the twenty-five bedraggled, exhausted men staggered down the cliff and onto the beach while Earl Toole recorded the event with his camera. Like many, McManus simply curled up on one of the hundreds of flat boulders that covered the beach and fell asleep, later describing it as being "as comfortable as any Beautyrest mattress."

A few hours later, the Coast Guard cutter *Northland* arrived, dropping anchor just beyond the pack ice. It was one of the prettiest sights McManus had ever seen. Then, a small boat from the *Northland* managed to work its way through the ice to the beach, and began ferrying men out to the cutter. They were given showers, dry clothes and an extravagant navy meal. After they were dropped at BE-2, navy Catalinas ferried the men to BW-1 where they were debriefed and later sent back to the U.S. to new assignments.

En route to BW-1, the Catalinas flew directly over the planes on the ice cap. McManus stared in awe at what would come to be known as the Lost Squadron, the largest forced landing and rescue in U.S. aviation history. The planes were arranged in a tidy semicircle, with

The rescued airmen pull alongside the Northland.

McManus's P-38 in the center and slightly ahead of the others, which angled in protectively toward his. They couldn't have deliberately landed on a spacious airfield in perfect conditions and ended up in better formation.

To Brad McManus it felt like the end of a very long and extraordinary adventure, a happy ending to a disastrous trip. He felt quite sentimental watching the planes become tiny specks and finally disappear into the whiteness of the ice cap. *That's the end of the whole mission*, he thought to himself. *Sayonara*.

A last view from the air of one of the B-17s.

The Mystery of the Bombsights

SHORTLY AFTER THE PILOTS AND CREW OF TOMCAT GREEN AND Tomcat Yellow were rescued in late July 1942, military officials decided to send a team to the site to retrieve valuable equipment and see whether a full-scale salvage was possible. Leading the mission was Major Norman Vaughan, an arctic expert who had accompanied Admiral Richard Byrd to the Antarctic in 1929 and was now stationed at Crystal 1, an air force base in northern Quebec.

Of the valuable equipment left behind in the planes, the most sensitive was a pair of top secret Norden bombsights, one in each B-17. According to Vaughan, when officials debriefed the pilots and crew they discovered that both of the bombsights had been left behind but only one had been destroyed. Vaughan was to retrieve or destroy the other before Nazi scavengers arrived.

Vaughan, traveling by dogsled, and Max Demarest, an experienced cold-weather specialist, on skis, set out for the crash site at the end of August but storms delayed their progress. Finally, running low on provisions and with a ship scheduled to meet them at a remote location on the coast, Demarest returned, leaving Vaughan to continue alone.

As Vaughan tells the story, the self-destructing device had been activated on one of the bombsights but the second remained intact. Freeing it from its mount, he loaded it on his sled. The only other item he removed from the site was a brand-new .45-caliber pistol that one of the crew members had left behind.

Later, after Vaughan had left, military reports show that Max Demarest led an expedition to the planes. Confusing the issue is an inventory of recovered items dated August 27–30, 1942, that includes two bombsights. Vaughan, who later wrote a report that included a proposal for salvaging the planes with the help of personnel

Student bombardiers carry a Norden bombsight to their plane under armed escort.

at a nearby weather station, says that either Demarest or someone else may have been referring to the Norden bombsight frames or some kind of electrical instruments that they confused with a bombsight.

Decades later, Oran Earl Toole, the young radio operator in Crockett's rescue party, would accuse Vaughan of getting it wrong. According to an entry in Toole's 1942 log dated July 24, 9:30 A.M.: "...could see fellows from planes straggling in by pairs down the side of the mountain...made coffee ashore for them and they turned in dead tired. Brought bombsights down to launch. Only equipment outside of clothing and few rations salvaged from planes."

Although Toole admits that he doesn't remember seeing the bombsights himself and he didn't help unload the sled, he's certain Crockett would have brought them both out (or at least one of them, if it's true that the second bombsight had already been destroyed). Toole concedes that although he's searched military archives he's never found any formal documents, such as memos or debriefing reports, to prove or disprove his version.

PART TWO

THE SEARCH

CHAPTER TWO

YOU HAVEN'T FAILED UNTIL YOU QUIT

THE MORNING OF SATURDAY, AUGUST 1, 1981, was balmy, the temperature on its way to a scorching eighty-five degrees. On the tarmac at Atlanta's DeKalb-Peachtree Airport, Pat Epps and Richard Taylor helped Russell Rajani and his partner, Roy Degan, pack a twin-engine Piper Aztec with camping gear, food supplies, metal detectors, winter parkas and snow boots. To the aviation workers passing by the plane, it looked like a carefully planned arctic expedition. Anyone with experience in the Far North would have described it as inadequate for a winter camping weekend in northern Vermont. Epps's eldest brother, Ben, a retired airline

pilot, couldn't resist a crack as he watched the last piece of luggage, a cooler, being loaded on board: "You boys takin' ice to the Eskimos, huh?"

Years later Taylor would admit that their naïveté was astounding. "We brought hokey little sleeping bags, a four-man tent that slept one and a half, and a shovel," he observed wryly. "No spare gas tank or radio. We were just winging it, and we were lucky we didn't get into serious trouble."

In the four months since Epps had first called Rajani about finding the lost planes, an agreement had been roughed out. Rajani had the salvage rights, and he and Degan had already put a great deal of their

Russell Rajani, Richard Taylor, Pat Epps and Roy Degan pose in front of a Cessna at Sondre Stromfjord in Greenland. (Opposite) Aloft over the east coast of Greenland.

own time and money into researching the 1942 crash landing — talking to Danish government officials in Copenhagen, visiting military archives and locating and interviewing surviving pilots and crew members. So Epps and Taylor would each contribute $7,500 to finance the trip and Epps would take care of the flight arrangements through Epps Aviation and by borrowing his brother Doug's Aztec. Anything they salvaged would be split fifty-fifty.

"Planning a trip to the Arctic from Atlanta," Taylor would say reflectively, "takes a couple of days." That was the way Epps and Taylor liked to operate — informally, spontaneously, keeping bothersome details to a minimum, the better to plunge feetfirst into an adventure without having all the fun scheduled out of it. "Epps and I have a history of doing stuff this way," said Taylor, who was the self-appointed chronicler of everything they did. "Maybe not planning it out as well as it should be planned, but doing it anyway and figuring it out as we go."

A native of Washington, D.C., Taylor was a successful architect who was active in the Boy Scout movement and other civic

Richard Taylor rides through Sondre Stromfjord, one of their stopovers in Greenland.

organizations. His hobby was racing motorcycles — the only obvious link to his difficult teenage years. An indifferent student, Taylor had been a tall, gangly boy with a poor complexion and a greasy ducktail haircut who emulated James Dean in *Rebel Without a Cause.* He fought with his authoritarian father and later, when he joined the army in 1955, struggled with military discipline. (He rose to the rank of sergeant, but was discharged as a corporal.) By the early 1960s, when he attended Georgia Tech on a scholarship, he'd settled down and discovered in architecture a focus for his energies.

Epps was built like a fireplug, his square poker face betrayed by mischievous blue eyes. He had been raised in rural Georgia, and upon first meeting he could be mistaken for a "good ol' country boy" — naïve, even simpleminded. Epps looked that part completely, but he played it for effect. He was the son of Ben Epps, one of Georgia's aviation pioneers; photographs hanging on the walls of Epps Aviation showed his father alongside homemade flying machines (constructed from wires, fabric and bicycle parts), which he regularly crashed. Graduating from Georgia Tech in the mid-fifties with a degree in mechanical engineering, Epps joined the air force. He became a transport pilot and later worked as an engineer at a missile site in New Mexico. By the mid-1960s, he had founded his own business training pilots and servicing aircraft. Like his father, he was resourceful and audacious.

On August 2, when the four men reached Sondre Stromfjord on the west coast of

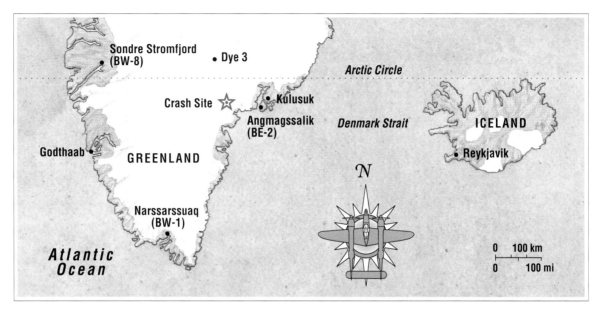

From Sondre Stromfjord on the west coast, they flew east, first to where the Lost Squadron had gone down, then on to Kulusuk, the nearest airfield and not far from Angmagssalik, home of the wartime base BE-2.

Greenland, Rajani and Degan transferred their gear into a small ski-equipped Cessna 185 rented from the local flying club, pilot included. With Epps and Taylor following in the Aztec, they flew across the ice cap to the east coast. According to Rajani's research, the Lost Squadron site was approximately ten miles inland. Locating an island ten miles offshore, he lined up the 1942 coordinates, set the course and timed the flight to the coast. It took four and a half minutes. Then, having adjusted his computations to take the wind into account, the pilot flew for the same duration inland. At the four-and-a-half-minute mark Rajani dropped a flare, and the two planes began circling the ice cap.

Epps and Taylor peered down. The landscape was a gently rolling, featureless blanket of whiteness. They had heard reports that the planes had been seen from the air as recently as 1961. A B-17 tail fin was twenty feet high, so there was every reason to believe the tip might be visible poking through a mound of snow. But they saw nothing. The

Cessna landed and dropped off Rajani and Degan. Then both planes flew to Kulusuk, a coastal airfield about forty minutes northeast, where Epps and Taylor boarded the Cessna.

Epps had assumed that a pilot from a Greenland flying club would be like an experienced bush pilot with 40,000 hours logged and a trail guide's knowledge of the ice cap. Their pilot, a laconic young Dane named Hans, was barely twenty. As they

While Epps and Taylor circled in their aircraft, Degan and Rajani landed the ski plane on the crash site of the Lost Squadron.

Hans, their young pilot (above), dropped Epps and Taylor in the midst of the ice cap (below).

flew over the ice cap, Epps asked, "Hans, you've been over here many times?"

"I've never been over here," Hans replied.

"But you have many, many flying hours?"

"Yeah," Hans said. "I have four hundred."

"Do you have your instrument rating?" Epps persisted.

"No."

After Epps and Taylor unloaded their

gear at the site, Hans prepared to take off. "Now you is nowhere," he said cheerfully. "G'day."

There was a light wind, but it wasn't as cold as they'd expected. It was a glorious day, the sun high and bright. Everywhere they looked there were two colors: glistening oyster gray and sparkling white. For men accustomed to the constant low-level hum of urban America, the silence was awesome. This was nature at its most elemental and majestic, and it affected them deeply. They dug a hole and put up their tent. When it proved to be too cramped for all their gear, they snapped two military ponchos together, creating an extension they called the South Wing.

It was certainly a fine spot for winter camping, but Rajani wasn't sure whether his seat-of-the-pants navigating had

Camp that summer of 1981 was a single tent, so cramped that their equipment had to be kept outside, under two outstretched ponchos.

brought them to the site of the forced landing. He and Degan began studying photographs of the downed planes taken in 1942, trying to match them to their surroundings.

Rajani, an Italian American born and raised in Chicago, was tall and lanky, a year shy of forty. As a carrier pilot he'd flown more than one hundred combat missions in A-7 fighters during the Vietnam War. He became a member of the Silkworm Club — an honor bestowed on pilots who save their lives by parachute — after ejecting from his fighter on Christmas Day, 1969, shortly before it plunged into the South China Sea. He identified strongly with the fraternity of fighter jocks and didn't have to be encouraged to talk about his military exploits. Later he became a commercial pilot with Republic Airlines. In the mid-1970s he decided to indulge in his longtime dream of recovering historic aircraft — especially World War II warbirds — and set up a corporation, Pursuits Unlimited, to that end.

Rajani came across the story of the Lost Squadron while reading a history of the P-38. In 1977, while on a business trip in Washington, D.C., he was driving past the

Danish embassy and impulsively dropped in. He learned that a California restaurateur and warbird collector had acquired salvage rights in 1974 but never acted on them. He began writing letters to the Danish government, arguing that it was time to give someone else a chance.

Rajani had met Degan, a Republic Airlines captain, while flying as his copilot earlier that year. The silver-haired Degan, a retired air force colonel and former director of operations for the Tennessee Air National Guard, stood six feet four and weighed more than two hundred pounds. He was a gregarious man, a salty storyteller who could keep a crowd spellbound with tales of piloting B-26 bombers over Korea or hauling cargo through antiaircraft fire in Vietnam. It was watching a P-38 streak overhead when he was ten years old that had inspired Degan to become a pilot. He flew vintage planes at air shows and had restored a grass airstrip near his Memphis home.

When Rajani mentioned the names of the P-38 pilots, Degan said he knew Carl Rudder, the former commander of Dobbins Air Force Base, just outside Atlanta.

For urban Americans, the emptiness and silence of Greenland were a shock.

Why didn't they go and talk to him? To Rajani, Degan was a godsend. Rajani had been conducting research and trying to raise financing in his limited free time. Degan had energy to spare. Together they combed military archives, interviewed anyone they could find who knew about the planes and met with government officials in Copenhagen. In May 1981 the salvage rights were transferred to Pursuits Unlimited for a two-year period, with the understanding that a B-17 would eventually be donated to a Danish aviation museum.

"Here it is," Rajani shouted. Lying behind one of the B-17s in a 1942 photograph was a distinctive-looking hill of bare rock. Beyond it, in the distance, was a range of mountains. Rajani and Degan found a vantage point from which they could see both landmarks approximately the way they appeared in the photos. "At least we know this is the spot," Rajani announced.

To help them find the planes, Epps and Taylor had rented a pair of magnetometers, devices that can detect iron and steel by the variations they cause in the earth's magnetic field. For practice they had walked around DeKalb-Peachtree Airport locating

Roy Degan using one of the magnetometers.

pipes under its concrete apron. The magnetometers had worked like a charm. On the ice cap, Epps and Taylor set up a simple grid pattern and the four men took turns walking in parallel lines about fifty yards apart. They took readings at regular intervals and watched for large fluctuations that might indicate the location of a plane. Once, Taylor's magnetometer registered a dramatic rise.

"Hey," he yelled to Epps. "Come here. I've got it!"

"I can't," Epps yelled back. "I've got something. You come here!"

Taylor quickly piled snow into a small cairn to mark his spot and ran to Epps. By the time he arrived, Epps's reading was flat. The two men ran back to Taylor's magnetometer and took a reading. It too was flat. A few minutes later Taylor would get a rise again. This happened countless times. The next day they retraced part of the grid to compare readings and got wildly different results. At the end of the day they puzzled over their data and reread the user's manual. Once they took two readings just minutes apart while sitting in their tent and the results were different. Nonetheless, something was happening and there was every reason to believe that the cause could be buried planes.

Finally they gave up on the magnetometer and dug an eight-foot hole to examine the characteristics of the densely packed ice. Ice lenses — layers in the ice that look like the rings in a tree — were plainly visible. "Each one must represent a summer thaw," Taylor deduced, drawing on his Boy Scout forest lore. He measured

Pat Epps digs in.

them and found they were about eighteen inches apart. If, like tree rings, each lens represented a year, he concluded, the planes were about forty feet deep.

Everyone was stunned by the idea. If Taylor's findings were correct, digging down to a plane was going to be a far more ambitious excavation project than they had expected.

On the third day Hans was supposed to pick them up, but he didn't appear at the arranged time. It was overcast, they told themselves, not the kind of weather to go looking for four tiny figures on the ice cap. The next day was clear, but still no Hans. Epps was growing especially agitated since he'd left his credit card and the Aztec as collateral. The adventure was over and they were ready to leave, and the ice cap was fast becoming inhospitable. Yet they had no idea whether anyone other than Hans knew where they were. What if Hans were lost? What if he'd crashed? Maybe he'd decided he was sick of Greenland and caught a last-minute flight to Denmark.

It was their first brush with the phenomenon of "arctic time": nothing happens quickly or on schedule. They were

relieved when they finally heard the drone of the Cessna approaching. Hans was right on schedule — arctic time.

BACK IN ATLANTA THE EXPEDITION attracted some media attention. An August 10 *Atlanta Constitution* article, for example, pictured the adventurers leaning against the wing of the Aztec and quoted Degan as saying, "The indications that we got from the magnetometers are so strong...there's no doubt in my mind that we located three airplanes. I am elated." In other stories, Epps, Taylor and Rajani put equally optimistic spins on the outcome of the trip, even though this wasn't how they would remember it. In fact, hairline fractures were appearing in the relationship between Rajani, who was nervous about losing control of the project, and Epps and Taylor, whose gung-ho approach sometimes overwhelmed people with whom they worked.

"I was disillusioned," Rajani said. "Epps and Taylor wanted to say we found the planes. I don't like to string anybody along, I like to tell it like it is. The photos proved we were in the area, but where are the planes? How deep are they, if they're still there? What if they've moved? What condition are they in?"

"When we got back," recalled Taylor, "Rajani and Degan started telling the world we'd found the planes. Pat and I didn't like this attitude."

For most of the fall, though, the relationship remained amicable. The contract Epps and Taylor had signed with Rajani expired at the end of the year. Rajani wanted them to raise $50,000 by that time, a sum he figured would compensate him for all his time and efforts to date. Otherwise he would seek investors elsewhere.

But to attract investors — let alone a line of bank credit — for so outlandish a scheme wasn't easy. Someone would have to be willing to take a flier that would make gold mines and board games look like blue-chip, Fortune 500 stock. They believed their best bet was to return to the ice cap in the fall to pinpoint the location of the planes.

In September Epps received a letter from a retired air force officer named Crocker Snow, who during World War II had been in charge of all North Atlantic aircraft and bases. Snow had seen a news clipping about the Greenland expedition and wrote that his brother-in-law, Norman Vaughan, had taken part in a salvage operation that retrieved equipment from the downed planes in August 1942. Norman was possibly the last person to see the Lost Squadron on the surface of the ice cap, and he wanted to get involved.

Epps did some computations in his head. Vaughan was probably in his late sixties, a little old to be taken on a strenuous trip to Greenland but certainly worth talking to. He decided to call him. Epps asked Vaughan whether he knew where the planes were. Vaughan told him he knew their approximate location. Epps asked him whether he thought he could find them again. Vaughan said he couldn't guarantee that, since he thought they'd be under the snow, but he would be an invaluable asset to any expedition. Over the course of

several phone conversations, Epps side-stepped the issue of whether he was willing to take Vaughan to Greenland.

"It's cold up there," Epps said.

"I live in Anchorage," Vaughan replied. "I know how cold it is."

"But it's kind of out in the wilderness," Epps said.

"I know what wilderness is."

Finally Epps asked, "Mr. Vaughan, how old are you?"

"Hell, sonny, I'm seventy-six years old," Vaughan told him. "I handled the sled dogs on Admiral Byrd's expedition to Antarctica in 1929. I drove a dog team across the glacier to those planes in '42. I take part in the big sled-dog race across Alaska every year...."

Vaughan lived in Alaska but was visiting relatives in Boston. Since Epps Aviation had a contract with the Federal Reserve to haul canceled checks from various U.S. cities, Epps arranged for

Norman Vaughan at the time of his trip with Byrd to Antarctica.

Vaughan to catch one of his Learjets to Atlanta. After meeting him, Epps and Taylor were convinced. Besides being vigorously fit for his age and knowledgeable about the Arctic, Vaughan was a charming character.

The son of a prosperous Boston tanner, he had dropped out of Harvard in 1925 to drive sled dogs in Newfoundland for Dr. Wilfred Grenfell, the famed British missionary. Four years later Vaughan joined Byrd's first expedition to Antarctica. Later he became an advertising executive and was a member of the U.S. dogsled team at the 1932 Winter Olympics at Lake Placid, the only year the Olympics featured that event. During World War II he joined the Army Air Corps as an arctic specialist, rising to the rank of lieutenant colonel. One of his missions was to travel by dogsled to the Greenland crash site to retrieve equipment from the B-17s and P-38s. After the war he sold chain saws and snowmobiles but didn't enjoy the business world. In the mid-1970s he moved to Alaska, where he worked at odd jobs while seeking sponsors for adventures. A restless soul, by 1981 Vaughan had been divorced three times. He was a living part of the history of the planes, and Epps and Taylor felt an immediate kinship with him. Even though Vaughan had no money to invest, they figured he might help attract investors. Epps asked him to join their next expedition, scheduled for October.

To try to solve the puzzle of their wildly erratic magnetometer readings, Epps and Taylor visited the experimental station at the Georgia Institute of Technology, their alma mater. They were told that the fluctuations in their readings were probably caused by solar disturbances and by the generally intense magnetic activity common at high latitudes. Subsurface radar would probably be more effective. A few suggested contacts led to a Philadelphia-based geophysicist named Bruce Bevan, who agreed to accompany them to the ice cap for a modest fee.

To raise money for the October trip, which was going to cost about $25,000, Epps canvassed customers, business associates and friends. He found ten people willing to invest $2,500 each. Most wrote him checks. One man, a longtime customer, lent him his Cessna Citation, a sleek corporate jet that seated eight, in exchange for maintenance work.

On October 18 Epps, Taylor, Rajani,

The American radar station Dye 3. A ski-plane dropped Epps, Taylor, Vaughan and others here in October 1981, on their way to the crash site.

Vaughan and Bevan flew to Greenland with more than 1,600 pounds of gear, of which Bevan's subsurface radar equipment accounted for half. Four days later, after being held up by bad weather, they departed Sondre Stromfjord on board a ski-equipped Greenland Air Twin Otter. Their destination was Dye 3, one of the chain of radar stations, built during the Cold War, that stretched from Alaska to Greenland. A measure of how they were feeling was reflected in Taylor's diary entry that day: "There's a feeling that always comes over you at this point in an undertaking like this. It has the elements of an inner satisfaction coupled with a sense of anxiety. You feel that you've overcome a neverending series of hurdles and there is nothing but success ahead."

Instead they hit an insurmountable hurdle: the weather. Storms buffeted the ice-cap site, and reports called for more of the same. The expedition was canceled and the disappointed men returned to Sondre Stromfjord.

Undiscouraged, Norman Vaughan boards the Cessna after bad weather forced them to cut short their October 1981 trip.

After settling their hotel and fuel bills, Epps and Taylor, feeling utterly defeated, began loading their gear into the Cessna. Beside them Vaughan whistled a cheerful tune under his breath. Finally Taylor said, "I don't know what you're so happy about, Norman. We've failed."

"We haven't failed until we quit," Vaughan said, staring at Taylor quizzically. "We're not quitting, are we?"

Epps and Taylor exchanged glances and said in unison, "No way."

WHEN EPPS AND TAYLOR WERE UNABLE to raise the $50,000 by New Year's Day, 1982, their contract with Rajani lapsed. They were, however, no less obsessed with finding the Lost Squadron and, confident they would reach a new agreement with Rajani, began planning another expedition to Greenland while continuing to search for backers. Rajani, meanwhile, also went looking for money. He approached Lockheed, the company that had designed and built the P-38, and Boeing, maker of the B-17. He went to Washington to meet air force officials and visit the National Science Foundation. He contacted an assortment of wealthy individuals interested in aviation, and he got in touch with corporations that might see in the project a marketing and public-relations opportunity. The response was always the same: Fascinating story. Sorry we're unable to help.

Several times during the first half of the year, Epps prepared new agreements for Rajani to sign. In each case Rajani, while signaling his willingness to make a deal, demanded revisions. Gradually relations between Rajani and the Greenland Expedition Society (GES), as Epps and Taylor now called themselves, grew increasingly tense. Finally things turned ugly.

In preparation for the upcoming expedition, Norman Vaughan had been living in Atlanta since April, operating out of a small office at Epps Aviation. According to him, on July 9, Rajani went through private papers on Vaughan's desk and stole several valuable 1942 photographs of the downed aircraft that belonged to GES. Rajani said that Vaughan had sent him the photographs with instructions to use them as he wished; Vaughan countered that Rajani had only been sent blurry photocopies to stimulate his interest in concluding contract negotiations. At some point Rajani tried to lure Vaughan on an expedition he was planning without Epps and Taylor since Vaughan's relationship with those two was based on a handshake rather than formal contracts. An old-fashioned man, Vaughan was offended that Rajani thought he would break his word. (The dispute became so confused that years later no one involved can accurately remember the details.)

Early in August Rajani filed two lawsuits against GES. ("He sued Epps, Taylor and me for a million dollars!" Vaughan hooted. "Greatest compliment I've ever had because I don't have a red dime.") Although the suits were later dismissed, they forced GES to delay and finally abandon the trip. But Epps, Taylor and Vaughan knew that Rajani and Degan were themselves preparing to leave for Greenland in two weeks, and that Rajani was having discussions with a potential corporate backer, the R. J. Reynolds Tobacco Company. It seemed to the three men that Rajani had acted in bad faith and was trying to squeeze them out. On August 13, Vaughan swore out a warrant against Rajani for "theft of trade secrets," and the sheriff's office threw Rajani in jail for several hours until he could locate a lawyer and obtain bail. (The matter eventually reached the federal courthouse in Atlanta, where a judge bluntly told them to work it out themselves — another way of telling them not to waste valuable court time with petty wrangles.)

While Rajani was tied up with GES, Degan took his youngest son, a couple of friends and Bruce Bevan to Greenland in a corporate jet, then spent a couple of days making ground-level passes over the ice cap with Bevan's radar equipment attached to the underside of a small ski-plane. Blizzards and 100-mile-per-hour winds ended the modest expedition, but the local media still ran stories on Degan when he returned. All the publicity irked Rajani, even though it was Degan's efforts that had indirectly led to the R. J. Reynolds connection.

Degan had been trying to persuade his friend Fred Smith, the Memphis millionaire who had founded Federal Express, to sponsor an expedition. Although the deal never materialized, word of Federal Express's interest made its way across the country to a Los Angeles restaurateur and amateur adventurer who would soon become an active player.

Jay Fiondella owned Chez Jay, a tiny

celebrity hangout in Santa Monica with bowls of peanuts on the bar and sawdust on the floor. Its customers included Marlon Brando, Warren Beatty, Henry Kissinger, Frank Sinatra, Robert Redford and astronaut Alan Shepard, who in 1971 took a Chez Jay peanut to the moon. And it was said that in 1971 Daniel Ellsberg, who was working at a nearby government think tank, passed the Pentagon Papers to a *New York Times* reporter at a back table.

An occasional actor in TV shows and movies, the fifty-six-year-old Fiondella was also a hot-air balloonist and treasure-hunter. His most famous expedition was a 1973 effort to recover a fortune said to be lost aboard the Italian luxury liner *Andrea Doria*, which sank off the Massachusetts coast in the mid-1950s. (Divers found some silverware and a bottle of perfume.) Sometimes described as an Indiana Jones figure, Fiondella was the embodiment of the go-for-broke-but-always-have-fun California entrepreneur. His motto was "Dreamers live forever; toilers die tomorrow." He was also fond of introducing himself by saying, "Hi, my real name is Jay Pigeon. You name it, I've lost money on it."

In the late 1960s Fiondella heard about the Lost Squadron from an airline pilot who was a regular customer at Chez Jay. As a Seabee (naval construction worker) stationed in the Pacific during World War II, Fiondella had admired the sleek P-38s and met many of their pilots. He considered mounting an expedition to Greenland himself but decided it would be too expensive. When a friend told him that Federal Express was considering backing a couple of Georgia pilots who were after the planes, Fiondella contacted Degan and Rajani. "Look," he told them, "this should be filmed and I'm in the business. I'll bring along a cameraman and I'll be the sound man." When Rajani called back to tell him Federal Express had pulled out, Fiondella said, "I'm into treasure-hunting and exploration, and I get a lot of high-profile people in my restaurant. Let me work on it."

One of Fiondella's earliest heroes had been Lowell Thomas, of the New York–based Explorers Club. As a teenager he remembered hearing Thomas speak about how explorers often relied on corporate sponsorship to mount expeditions. Fiondella himself was often hired to fly hot-air balloons in commercials because many companies liked to associate their products with machismo and adventure. What, he thought, were the three most obvious products? Cars, alcoholic beverages…and cigarettes. That made Fiondella think of Ed Horrigan, president of the R. J. Reynolds Tobacco Company.

Fiondella knew Horrigan from their hometown of East Haven, Connecticut, where Horrigan had dated Fiondella's sister. Horrigan was a brash, hard-nosed businessman whose approach to corporate affairs was said to have been shaped by a Korean War experience when he had single-handedly stormed a machine-gun nest. He was also a high roller who might be seduced, rather than daunted, by an epic challenge. When Fiondella called him and proposed the idea, Horrigan asked for a presentation. Rajani flew to Los Angeles, and he and Fiondella met with Horrigan and several Reynolds executives at an exclusive Beverly Hills hotel. Rajani gave a forty-five-minute presentation, complete with slides and a written report, detailing the history of the Lost Squadron, the weather in Greenland, the logistics of reaching the ice cap and a three-phase plan: locating the planes, digging down to check on their condition, and removing them if they were worth restoring. Rajani explained that he couldn't estimate what it would cost to remove the planes until the first two phases were completed. His budget to locate and, if possible, dig down to a plane was $320,000.

The Reynolds executives were impressed with the idea. At first the proposal seemed a natural for their Camel brand of cigarettes, but Camel's promotional budget was too small for so costly a venture. Instead the project

was transferred to Winston, the company's flagship brand.

By 1982, although Reynolds was a diversified company with many holdings, manufacturing cigarettes was a $7-billion business and its greatest source of profits. But the industry was in trouble, and Reynolds was suffering. Health concerns about smoking meant declining demand and tougher government regulations. Winston, introduced in the mid-1950s as the first filter-tip cigarette, had been America's best-selling brand for nearly a quarter of a century. Having abandoned its familiar jingle, "Winston tastes good like a cigarette should," after cigarette ads were banned from radio and television in 1971, Winston failed to come up with an effective advertising campaign to replace it. Meanwhile competitor Philip Morris was increasing

Jay Fiondella (left) had first heard of the Lost Squadron in the sixties. When he learned that Russell Rajani (center) and Roy Degan (right) were also looking for it, he managed to interest the R.J. Reynolds Tobacco Company in sponsoring them to search for the planes.

market share for its Marlboro brand by building on a hugely successful campaign for Marlboro Country, a mythical wilderness inhabited by a rugged cowboy called the Marlboro Man.

In 1976 Marlboro overtook Winston as the market leader. Since then Reynolds had been trying to beat Philip Morris at its own game, introducing a "working men of America" theme that featured rugged outdoorsmen. According to a 1979 Federal Trade Commission report on cigarette advertising, "A Winston man was projected as 'a man's man who is strong, vigorous, confident, experienced, mature.'" The latest twist was an aviation theme featuring storm searchers and mountain patrol missions. What better marketing and promotional tie-in than the pursuit of real World War II planes on the Greenland ice cap?

The official crest of the Winston-sponsored expedition.

T HROUGHOUT LATE 1982 AND EARLY 1983, Rajani, Degan and Fiondella attended meetings in Winston-Salem, North Carolina, Reynolds's corporate hometown. Besides negotiating a contract and planning the expedition, they were being groomed by Reynolds for what had been dubbed the Winston Recovery Team.

In January Reynolds sent the three men to an arctic survival camp in Quebec. Later they attended a media course in New York that taught them to deflect questions about

the health concerns of cigarettes — none of them smoked, although Rajani began puffing occasionally for effect — and to mention the Winston Recovery Team at every opportunity. At public appearances they wore blue aviator shirts, red ties, gray slacks and lambskin flight jackets with the team logo — an eagle outlined in gold stitching — emblazoned over the right breast pocket. In one publicity photo Rajani and Fiondella are shown decked out in their Winston Recovery Team outfits and meeting with an elderly Clarence "Kelly" Johnson, designer of the P-38, at his California home.

As Rajani, Degan and Fiondella announced at a press conference in New York on February 23 (and during a ten-city publicity tour in March), Phase One of the expedition would establish a base camp and locate the planes with subsurface radar. Phase Two would involve giant C-130 aircraft delivering a bulldozer and other heavy snow-removal equipment that would excavate around the buried planes. ("We estimate the planes are buried under forty feet of snow," Fiondella told reporters. "The snow is like Styrofoam, so digging shouldn't be too hard.") Phase Three would be the arrival of a powerful helicopter capable of lifting an eight-ton P-38 and carrying it to a waiting freighter for delivery to the U.S. The expedition was scheduled to begin on June 1, 1983, to take advantage of Greenland's relatively mild summer months.

"A dream come true" was how Rajani described it at the press conference. "The Winston Recovery Team is the ideal sponsorship opportunity for Winston cigarettes,"

said one Winston executive. "It bonds fifteen men giving their personal best to help an adventurer accomplish his dream..."

Rajani was in charge of hiring the crew, which included mechanics, airframe specialists and a surveyor, as well as his lawyer, Tom McHugh, and his father-in-law. Since it was billed as an adventure, each crew member was paid $100 a week (plus all expenses), and many used vacation time or took leaves of absence. Rajani also hired a New Hampshire–based geophysical firm with experience in subsurface radar. Meanwhile, Reynolds satisfied insurance requirements by hiring a parallel support crew — consisting of arctic survival experts and a doctor — whose leader, Mike Weiss, could override Rajani.

As soon as he arrived in Greenland, Degan saw that Rajani's organization was haphazard at best (a view that came to be shared by many team members as the trip progressed). Rajani had leased a twin-engine ski-plane from Sondre Stromfjord in advance, but it was damaged in an accident the day before they arrived. Since there were no other available planes in Greenland and no backup arrangements had been made, a used ski-plane had to be purchased in Denmark. Essential items such as rope, snowshoes and long underwear were missing or in short supply, and the portable electrical system lacked a converter needed to run a vital steam machine. Supplies that should have been there when the crew arrived trickled in over two weeks. A Danish official who was present wondered aloud why Rajani hadn't bought most of the food supplies in Kulusuk, the coastal air base closest to the ice-cap site. Even though prices were much higher in

The Winston Recovery Team poses at the Atlanta airport before leaving for Greenland in May 1983.

73

Greenland, he pointed out, it cost even more to ship all the food via charter aircraft from the U.S., and the logistics were nightmarish.

While the Winston Recovery Team waited for a week in Kulusuk for the weather to clear and missing supplies to arrive, Rajani wasted no time in clashing with Mike Weiss. He accused Weiss, who had fractured a bone in his forearm while skiing on the day of his arrival, of reckless behavior that could jeopardize the expedition. Weiss in turn told Rajani that he made too many snap decisions without analyzing the facts, and then changed his mind constantly. The most ludicrous incident occurred on the fifth day, when the local law-enforcement official contacted Weiss and asked that any handguns be collected and held by the airport manager until their owners left Greenland. Rajani, who had brought four pistols — his own plus three he had purchased out of the Reynolds budget — was incensed. He accused Weiss of trying to take over the expedition and appealed to Degan, Fiondella and McHugh to oppose him. Weiss, who was responsible for safety, said he and his team would have to withdraw from the expedition if Rajani didn't turn over his weapons.

Degan was amazed at Rajani. During their first visit to Greenland with Epps and Taylor in 1981, they had learned that while hunting rifles and shotguns were permitted, it was against customs regulations to bring handguns into Greenland. When neither Degan, Fiondella nor his own lawyer, McHugh, would support him, Rajani threatened to dissolve the entire expedition.

The next day Weiss told Degan that Rajani was childish, and that he found it nearly impossible to believe that the leader of a $500,000 project might shut it down because he couldn't tote his pistols around.

Finally, on their eighth day in Greenland, the crew landed on the ice cap. Relations between Rajani and Degan deteriorated badly. Degan was shocked to learn that Rajani, who intended to locate the planes using the coordinates alone, hadn't brought his 1942 photographs. When Degan pointed out that the hand-held sextants they were supposed to use to work out their positions weren't very accurate, Rajani dismissed his concerns. Later Rajani argued that Degan was upset that Winston had put him, a younger man, in charge of the expedition. He called Degan a publicity hound and complained that, having been given the important job of coordinating all air traffic to and from the ice cap, Degan petulantly refused to leave the site for fear he'd miss the discovery of the planes.

Degan felt the main reason Rajani was spending most of his time flying all over Greenland was to untangle all the problems caused by his own stream-of-consciousness planning. He also believed Rajani was doing all the flying himself in order to spend more time in the relative comfort of hotels in Sondre Stromfjord or Kulusuk rather than in a tent on the ice cap. Now Degan was convinced that Rajani and his main ally, McHugh, were trying to discredit him. On Thursday, June 16, he wrote in his journal, "Now I find out since they have made so many screw-ups on aircraft, on paper I have been put in charge.

(Top) After several delays, the Winston Recovery Team landed on the ice cap and set to work creating a snug camp built around the large mess building, prominently displaying the team logo. (Left) One of the first jobs was to begin erecting the ice wall to protect the personnel tents (bottom), which were set up around the main building.

(Above) Tents were not the only thing marked in keeping with the team's commercial function. Virtually all other equipment was in the official colors of red and blue.

The completed camp, surrounded by the protective ice wall and with the Winston flag snapping overhead.

I will not allow them to make me the scapegoat for all their screw-ups."

As leader of the survival crew, Weiss ordered that the camp be built and secured against storms before any salvage work began. A twenty-by-forty-foot wooden barracks that served as mess hall, communications center and first-aid station was put up, and the sleeping tents were pitched around it. Then Weiss formed teams to erect a giant windbreak made from ice blocks to protect the camp. Rajani opposed building the wall, and tried to encourage opposition to Weiss. But the bonding that the Reynolds executive had spoken of during the press conference did not include Rajani. Many of the crew members grew openly contemptuous of him, and several

complained to Degan that Rajani was arrogant and obnoxious. They talked about dropping their trousers and giving him a bare-assed salute the next time he flew in from Sondre Stromfjord on July 22.

A few days later a blizzard rolled in. As conditions worsened, with winds gusting to fifty miles per hour, Weiss began gathering help to work on the ice wall. He entered the barracks and called for assistance. "We've got a very serious situation out here with this storm," he said. "We need all the help we can get to work on the wall." Degan and a couple of others donned coats, gloves and goggles. Rajani, who was playing chess with McHugh as the walls shook and cans and bottles hit the floor, rolled his eyes and blew a raspberry in Weiss's direction. Weiss replied with an insult of his own and

When the camp was hit by one of Greenland's fierce blizzards, tensions that had been simmering between Rajani (left) and the rest of the recovery team erupted.

went back outside. Seconds later he and McHugh were battling it out in the blizzard. It took Degan and several others to pull the men apart.

Aside from the human conflicts, the radar equipment was malfunctioning almost daily. The planes still hadn't been located even though it was nearly the end of June. Degan was frustrated because the search was concentrated in an area that didn't conform to his methodical matching of ice-cap geography to the 1942 photographs. There was always an element of guesswork about locating your position on

the ice cap, but Degan felt Rajani was way off. One night, as he lay in his sleeping bag, he remembered Rajani telling the press that Man was involved in three types of conflict: Man against man, Man against machines and Man against the elements. So far, Degan thought, Man was being pummeled by all three.

Years later Fiondella would defend Rajani and the expedition. "Russ did the best he could," he said. "There's bickering and fistfights on most adventures I've ever read about. Personalities get strained. The wind was blowing all the time and we were up there for two months at the mercy of

Digging out after a storm. Despite the construction of the protective ice wall, Greenland's fierce storms still dumped several feet of snow on the camp.

radar operators whose equipment wasn't working."

Beyond individual squabbles, however, Rajani was in charge, and blunders occurred with a regularity that could not be accounted for by bad luck or an occasional error in judgment. By the end of July the Winston Recovery Team was in crisis. Probably the most dispiriting moment came when they discovered that more than two weeks of searching with subsurface radar had been a waste of time. While on one of his stays in Sondre Stromfjord, Rajani had met the crew of a P-3 Orion, the United States Navy's high-tech antisubmarine plane equipped with a sensitive magnetic anomaly detector intended to find submarines hundreds of feet below the ocean's surface. The pilot agreed to fly over the expedition site on his way to Iceland. The P-3 made several passes and reported positive readings. Something made of metal and large enough to register on the plane's equipment lay beneath the ice, although it was impossible to judge how deep or to pinpoint the location. It was an area that had already been covered by the subsurface radar, so Rajani asked the operators to take

their equipment over it again. Again they came up with nothing, even though Rajani had buried a shovel a few feet under the snow. (Although Rajani felt he'd proved a point, the operators were not to blame for failing this test. Subsurface radar cannot read objects buried so near the surface.)

The radar crew left as scheduled toward the end of the month with the planes still not located. A combination of low morale, boredom and the effects of the worst summer weather in recent history was turning the expedition into a disaster. Rajani and the remaining team members — many had already returned home to their families and jobs — flew to Iceland for a week-long holiday. By the time they returned to the ice cap, Rajani had brought in another subsurface radar crew and a geologist with a magnetometer, who searched for the planes without success. (One surprise visitor during this period was Norman Vaughan. After Richard Taylor made a passionate pitch to R. J. Reynolds that Vaughan was part of the history of the Lost Squadron, the company agreed to send him for a short visit, against Rajani's wishes.) By the end of the month, R. J. Reynolds had canceled the expedition, authorizing a skeleton crew to shut down the camp.

Desperate to salvage what was left of the project, Rajani hired a team of glaciologists from the University of Iceland. Helgi Bjoernsson and his technicians, Jon Sveinsson and Addi Hermannsson, had designed and built a subsurface radar device they called the Icescope. As Bjoernsson explained to Rajani, most subsurface radar used high-frequency signals in the 120 MHz range.

(Top) With his radar crews unable to locate anything buried under the ice, an increasingly desperate Rajani convinced the crew of a navy Orion to fly over their site to see whether their plane's sophisticated equipment could detect anything that might be the lost aircraft. (Left) Jay Fiondella under the Orion's tail at Sondre Stromfjord.

(Above) Finally, Rajani brought in Professor Helgi Bjoernsson from Reykjavik, who brought with him a specially designed subsurface radar he called the Icescope (bottom).

Such systems worked well on polar glaciers, in which there was no melting water, but could not penetrate temperate glaciers (the type found in Greenland and Iceland), which were made up of ice and water. The Icescope operated on a much lower frequency (in the 5 MHz range), and Bjoernsson had been successfully using the device to survey glaciers for Icelandic hydroelectric studies. In one instance he identified some unusual reflections as being a plane that had crashed in the area three decades earlier.

A one-of-a-kind system, Bjoernsson's Icescope looked as though Rube Goldberg had designed it for an alpine soapbox derby. Housed in a boxy single-seat wooden sled mounted on skis, the radar faceplate resembled World War II communications equipment — an oscilloscope surrounded by knobs, dials and meters. Electromagnetic waves directed through the ice bounced back, either off bedrock or any objects in their path. A Yashica autodrive camera had been attached to record the oscilloscope's fluorescent screen on film, which the Icelanders developed and studied after every survey. A bicycle wheel rigged to the back of the sled synchronized distances on an odometer so a positive reading could be pinpointed later. The antennae dragged along the snow several yards behind, like a dawdling child.

Bjoernsson and his team began taking readings on July 27. Although they turned up some suspicious reflections that first day, they lacked enough data to draw any conclusions. Then, on the evening of Monday, August 1, they located two large metal objects. Two days later they located six more, and the pattern conformed to the positions of the aircraft in 1942. Since the Icescope was imprecise at measuring depth, Bjoernsson could only estimate the objects to be at least one hundred feet down. In an effort to obtain a core sample, the crew used one-inch hose with a copper-tipped nozzle attached to a high-pressure steamer to bore a hole eighty-eight feet deep. (Later Bjoernsson revised his estimate to two hundred feet deep, maybe more.) Before they left the ice cap, Rajani marked the location of each P-38 with empty fuel drums and erected a twenty-foot metal tower on a wooden platform over one of the B-17s.

A postmortem report prepared for R. J. Reynolds by the company's public-relations department noted that the Winston Recovery Team was, "from a public relations point of view, a successful program." As of the end of September 1983, stories on the expedition had been carried by 369 newspapers, 31 television stations, 27 radio stations and 11 national magazines. Using the magic of modern information-gathering, Reynolds documented 131 million "news media impressions." Nearly 3 million listeners heard about the expedition on radio, and another 4.6 million viewers saw television coverage.

Nonetheless, the results from the ice cap were inconclusive — even though objects that seemed likely to be the planes had been located — and the dissension made it hard for the PR department to "create the aura of an adventure conducted by 15 men working together as a team." A dozen journalists — including representatives from

People magazine and the nationally syndicated television show "That's Incredible" — were scheduled to visit the site when the first plane was unearthed but, according to the report, "because of a lack of dramatic findings on the ice cap, the media trip was cancelled [and] plans for a documentary were also shelved." The postexpedition press conference was held in Atlanta "because the Atlanta media had shown the most interest in the expedition and we wanted to minimize the fact that the planes were not brought back to the United States as planned."

As a philosophical Fiondella put it, "It's always a little disappointing when you aren't able to complete something you start. But you know, the ice cap doesn't give up its treasures very easily."

IN 1984 RAJANI CONVINCED A NATURAL-GAS tycoon from Texas to underwrite a modest $30,000 expedition that took readings and made observations. The following year Fiondella obtained Rajani's permission

to mount an expedition on his rights. He created a nonprofit foundation called the Historical Aircraft Recovery Team (HART) and persuaded a group of San Francisco lawyers and businesspeople to invest a total of $200,000, with the promise that they would receive a P-38 if the planes were excavated.

Fiondella enlisted Burt Avedon, whom he'd met through his association with the Explorers Club. Avedon, a former World War II ace and navy test pilot, was president of Willis & Geiger, one of the world's oldest expedition outfitters. Then one of the investors put Fiondella in touch with Seattle-based Ray Cox, whose company, Western World Retrievals, specialized in finding aircraft. Cox in turn hired Joe Tuttle, an avionics expert, to organize the technology needed to locate the planes. Assuming Canadians would know something about finding things under snow and ice, Tuttle contacted the Geological Survey of Canada, a federal agency responsible for all of the country's geophysical exploration. If you want an expert, Tuttle was told, contact William "Bil" Thuma.

Thuma, a short, solidly built forty-year-

(Left) In 1985, Jay Fiondella returned to the ice with a group known as HART. The search for the planes continued, using radar and (right) even more traditional divining techniques.

The easiest way to find the aircraft Bjoernsson had located in 1983 was to locate the twenty-foot tower the Winston Recovery Team had erected over what they thought was a B-17.

old with a degree in geophysical sciences from Michigan Tech, began his career working mainly in mining exploration, eventually moving to Toronto to work for a giant copper producer. Over the years, he began to spend more time developing and marketing geophysical technology. His hobby was archaeology, and tracking down historical planes intrigued him, so when Tuttle asked him if he'd like to look for the Lost Squadron, Thuma agreed.

Following the coordinates, the HART expedition landed on the ice cap on September 11, 1985. There was no sign of the previous camps or the twenty-foot tower. Finding the tower, they agreed, was their first objective, since it was supposed to be located over a B-17, the largest target. After setting up camp, the men tried to find the tower using photographs, surveying instruments and satellite navigation equipment. When that failed, they tried intuition and curses. Nine days later, having endured a sudden and fierce blizzard, Thuma picked up a magnetic anomaly on his magnetometer. Using a chain saw plugged into a portable generator, Cox sliced into the snow and hit the tip of the tower at a depth of six inches.

Since the aircraft were made of many ferromagnetic components — that is, mainly iron and steel — Thuma knew they should create an anomaly in the earth's natural magnetic field that his high-sensitivity magnetometer would pick up. After digging out the tower, which would cause interference, Thuma and the crew set up a grid and crisscrossed the site. What if the radar findings by the Icelanders were inaccurate? Since glaciers are huge masses of ice that flow slowly downhill, the men knew the planes would have drifted in the more than four decades since the landing, but how far? Claiming he could hear the distant rumbles of icebergs breaking off the glacier at the coast, Avedon, in an account published in the Explorers Club journal, wrote that sooner or later "an iceberg would calve off...with a B-17 or P-38

on top for a hood ornament..."

Intense magnetic storms disrupted Thuma's surveys for several days. By the end of the expedition on September 24, the HART crew had excavated three empty 55-gallon fuel drums, five jerry cans filled with gasoline, a vinyl tub and several folding lawn chairs left by the 1983 Winston Recovery Team, but no airplanes.

A month later, having had the time to run his data through computers and review the findings patiently, Thuma was able to draw a tentative conclusion about what they called site number four, the B-17 tower, which put the plane at a far greater depth than anyone had imagined. In the report he submitted to Cox, Thuma wrote, "it seems plausible that the aircraft at Site #4 is at a depth of 258' (78.6 m)."

Thuma never heard from Cox, Fiondella or anyone else associated with the expedition. Eventually he decided they must have run out of money, lost interest or lost the salvage rights. It would be three years before Thuma would be contacted by the Greenland Expedition Society and discover how remarkably accurate his estimate was.

Bil Thuma tried to pinpoint where the planes had crashed by matching the surrounding mountains with those visible in 1942 photographs.

CHAPTER THREE

HERE LIES BIG STOOP

FOR SEVERAL YEARS, OUT OF THE LOOP BUT still keenly interested, Epps and Taylor monitored the various expeditions that journeyed to Greenland and returned empty-handed. Some of their information came from Roy Degan who, after his difficulties with Rajani, became increasingly friendly with Epps and Taylor. After Degan and Norman Vaughan returned from the ice cap in 1983, stories circulated over drinks at the Downwind about how the Winston Recovery Team had been plagued by poor organization and leadership. (Early in 1984 Epps and Taylor approached R. J. Reynolds about backing another expedition but were politely rebuffed.) They took note that Rajani had not accompanied the expeditions in '84 or '85. Every few months Taylor would write or call his contact in the Danish government. "Just probing," he would say. "I wanted to see what the mood was like, whether there was an opportunity." By early 1986, sensing that Rajani's efforts were losing momentum, Epps and Taylor launched a full-scale campaign to win the salvage rights.

The Danes were receptive, so Taylor flew to Copenhagen in April. He was joined by Vaughan, who was visiting Europe at the time. The men argued that since Rajani had been given several years to get the planes and had failed, it was time to give the Greenland Expedition Society a chance. On April 10 Rajani's rights were canceled. Two weeks later, the rights were transferred to GES for a three-year period, leaving just enough time to organize a summer expedition.

First they had to find the money. When looking for funds, many adventurers set up nonprofit organizations to attract investors with tax write-offs. Not Epps and Taylor. "To set up a money-losing thing didn't sit right with Epps or me," said Taylor. "Somehow, if everything worked well and we got the planes out, it might return a handsome profit for everybody who'd put anything in." Instead they established GES as a for-profit Georgia corporation.

For-profit or not, as summer 1986 approached, GES was a corporation with no assets and no investors, and it needed approximately $70,000. That's when Epps, who had heard about the popularity of adventure travel vacations, came up with an inspired idea: charge volunteers for the privilege of accompanying them to the ice cap and working for free. Not surprisingly, most of the people who bit were friends and family eager to help out. Epps raised

(Opposite) Pat Epps prepares for a takeoff in wet snow. Two expedition members rock the Cessna's wings to work the skis loose from the sticky snow.

$35,000 by collecting $5,000 each from a group that included his son, Patrick, Jr., his brother Doug, Doug's daughter Susan, and a couple of longtime customers of Epps Aviation who saw the expedition as a lark.

Epps and Taylor supplied the rest of the money. Epps's contribution was mainly equipment and services. In Halifax, for example, he bought a single-engine Cessna 185 equipped with skis to ferry people and supplies to and from the ice cap. But the nearly $18,000 price tag was too much for Taylor. He had family responsibilities. He also had a growing architectural partnership that had branched into the expensive business of buying land and then building condominiums for sale. So, in a characteristically optimistic GES move, Taylor signed a note for his share, promising that when they retrieved and sold a plane, he would reimburse GES from his share of the profits.

On July 13, with Epps already in Canada purchasing the ski-plane, Taylor and Patrick Epps, Jr., took off from DeKalb-Peachtree Airport in Epps Aviation's Piper Navajo. It was five years since Epps and Taylor had last set foot on the ice cap, and Taylor felt a tremendous sense of exhilaration as the plane's wheels lifted off the runway. On their way north they stopped in Philadelphia to pick up Bruce Bevan, the geophysicist who had accompanied Epps, Taylor and Rajani on their unsuccessful trip to the ice cap in October 1981.

Bevan was a mild-mannered forty-three-year-old academic who had studied electrical engineering, before switching to geology and developing a specialty in archaeological geophysics. He didn't have a whole lot of experience searching for airplanes or working in the Arctic, but he had an attribute that Epps and Taylor valued more highly than any other: he was enchanted by the project and as a result charged them a modest $6,000 for his services.

In preparation for the trip, Bevan studied books and reports on Greenland and glaciology. Because the atmosphere and geology can affect surveying equipment in

The Piper Navajo flies over Greenland's mountains. On arrival in Greenland, they transferred to a ski-plane for the flight to the ice cap.

Richard Taylor searches for the planes with an electromagnetic induction meter.

different and unexplained ways, Bevan decided he would rely on three different systems to search for the aircraft.

One was a proton magnetometer. Although no one had been able to determine the precise amount of iron in the planes, Bevan felt sure there would be enough for the magnetometer to detect them at fifty feet, maybe more. He also brought an electromagnetic induction meter. This device wasn't specifically designed for finding metal, but metal objects would register a distinctive reading on it so long as they weren't too deep.

Finally there was a ground-penetrating radar system. Bevan knew that in 1983 the Icelandic scientists had picked up readings of what they believed were the planes using a very low-frequency system — something in the neighborhood of 5 MHz. Antennae pulled along the ground and transmitting at that frequency were designed to penetrate hundreds of feet or more, and usually custom-made at great expense. The question was, how deep were the planes? The Icelanders had suggested they were 180 to 240 feet below the surface, but no one really believed that was possible. Most estimates of the aircrafts' depth ranged from an optimistic forty feet—Epps and Taylor's figure when trying to woo investors—to sixty or eighty feet. So Bevan brought two antennae — one that operated at 180 MHz and another that operated at 120 MHz — which could in theory provide readings to about 200 feet and had the added advantage of

being light enough to be pulled by one or two men.

The question of depth was less important to Bevan than location. Although he didn't doubt that Epps and Taylor could find the general vicinity in which the planes had landed in 1942, as far as Bevan knew, no one had pinpointed where they lay under the ice. (Epps and Taylor didn't believe Rajani's claim to have found them with Bjoernsson in 1983 and they didn't know about Thuma's 1985 report.) Furthermore, there was a great deal of uncertainty in his mind as to how far the planes had drifted in forty-four years. From his research, he knew that although the ice cap appeared to be as solid as rock, it was moving, urged along under its own weight, toward the coast. But he didn't know the precise direction or speed. Although parts of Greenland had been extensively studied and documented, there was relatively little information about the east coast. What research there was, however, indicated that the glacier was likely moving in a southeasterly direction. If the planes moved with it, they could be a mile or more away from the original site.

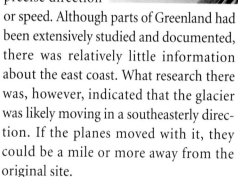

Bruce Bevan tinkers with his subsurface radar, which could find the planes at depths of up to two hundred feet.

On July 15, having calculated the 1942 crash site by shooting compass angles to distant mountain peaks, a dozen people representing the Greenland Expedition Society pitched their tents in shallow holes, constructed snow walls to protect them from the wind, and dug a trench for a latrine.

Then Taylor and several other expedition members started searching for the remains of the camp left by the Fiondella-Cox expedition the previous summer. Epps had learned that a twenty-foot wooden post had been left standing over one of the B-17s. On the evening of the second day, Taylor found it. It was sticking six inches above the ice cap, about a mile southeast of their camp.

That didn't necessarily mean that nearly twenty feet of snow had fallen, Taylor reasoned. For one thing, they didn't know how deep the post had been anchored. To withstand the high winds, it must have been sunk as much as half its height into the ice cap. Of course, Taylor didn't want to think what it would mean if even ten feet of snow had fallen annually over more than forty years. Besides, Taylor had always been struck by how the ice cap, far from being flat, was characterized by rolling dips and rises like the dunes of the Sahara Desert. Sometimes when the Cessna had to taxi for a mile or so while trying to take off on the wet, sticky snow, it would drop from sight only to reappear again on the next rise. Taylor, who had read everything he could about Lawrence of Arabia, recalled from one of the books that desert winds sometimes covered a village, then years later exposed it again. Could that explain why the planes had been seen as recently as the

The 1985 expedition had left a post over what they thought was a B-17.

1960s, then disappeared? In any event, their radar and magnetometer surveys over the area turned up only remnants of former campsites, but no sign of anything as large as an airplane.

Taylor and Bevan studied 1942 photographs of the planes and identified several promising survey areas. Bevan set up his ground-penetrating radar equipment on the plywood sled, the antennae trailing a few feet behind, and the work began. During the first week the sled was slowly dragged in parallel lines about fifty feet apart — a method roughly analogous to mowing a lawn — but turned up nothing. It was frustrating as well as back-breaking work, but one man's efforts quickly stood out.

Gordon Scott had paid $5,000 to join the expedition at the urging of his neighbor, Norman Vaughan. So far nearly everyone involved in the project had been family or friends, most of them from Georgia, which was the way Epps and Taylor liked it. They had created GES as a kind of *Boy's Own* adventure-in-the-Arctic, an extension of their trips to roll the pole or visit Mexican gold mines. Accepting strangers had demanded careful deliberation during board meetings at the Downwind. As Taylor would later drawl, "Pat and I weren't too anxious for it, but Gordon was a friend of Norman's. Then he came up with his money so he automatically qualified."

Scott instantly became an inner member of the fraternity. He was a big man, six feet six and weighing 220, with black hair and a black furry beard that made him look part wolf. A commercial fisherman by trade, Scott was an experienced mountain-climber

Gordon Scott pulling the subsurface radar.

Bruce Bevan and Richard Taylor examining a printout from the subsurface radar.

and skier who spent winters supervising rescue operations for one of Alaska's largest ski resorts. He was deliberate, determined and pensive, slow to talk, invaluable on the ice cap.

Aside from his physical strength and enormous energy, Scott had a remarkable ability to pace himself, adapting to whatever schedule hauling the sled demanded. He knew that at night, when the temperature dropped, the snow hardened underfoot, making it easier to pull the heavy sled. From then on, Scott frequently hauled during the day and then went out in the middle of the night to haul again. As Taylor pointed out, his patience was the marvel of the camp: "He knows how to keep his hopes up even when the fish aren't nibbling."

For the most part the expedition was blessed with good weather. Temperatures ranged from just below freezing to as high as forty degrees Fahrenheit with light winds under mainly clear skies. It was almost per-petual daylight; the sun dipped below the horizon for only four hours each night. There was enough sunlight to operate a simple solar water collector consisting of

dark polyethylene spread across a shallow trench. Melting ice supplied the camp with fresh water.

At around 2:00 A.M. on July 19, however, just a few hours after a gorgeous arctic sunset, the winds began gusting to fifty miles per hour from the direction of the high ice plateau in the interior. Norman Vaughan, who first recognized the sever-ity of the approaching storm, warned everyone to stay dressed and inside so their tents wouldn't blow away. Susan Epps, who had come along for the adventure and was sharing a tent with her father, Doug, was thankful she had built up their pro-tective snow wall the previous night. She and her father packed their belongings and weighted the corners of their tent.

The wind howled wildly all night, but thanks to Vaughan and Scott's supervision, the camp was secure. From time to time Susan or Doug would stick their video camera outside the tent to record the dra-matic scene. At one point Susan heard someone cursing loudly. In the morning she and her father discovered that Patrick Epps, Jr.'s tent had blown down, forcing

(Above left) July 19 was marked by a spectacular sunset. (Above right) Hours later, a severe blizzard hit.

(Opposite) When Gordon Scott got a reading that suggested something not far below the surface, expedition members began digging feverishly. After much hard work, they concluded sadly that Scott had detected an air pocket, not a plane.

him to seek shelter with Vaughan. The food storage tent was buried under several feet of snow. The wind whipped and wailed for another eighteen hours before the weather cleared. As far as adventure travel went, Epps, Jr., later said, "We was getting our money's worth."

With less than a week remaining, Vaughan asked Epps and Taylor to let him contact Helgi Bjoernsson in Reykjavik and bring him to the ice cap. Epps and Taylor were at first reluctant. They associated Bjoernsson with Rajani, for whom they had little respect. And since they doubted that Rajani had located the planes in 1983, they were equally skeptical of the scientist whose findings supposedly supported him. Vaughan, however, had met Bjoernsson and been impressed. Roy Degan flew Norman out to Kulusuk, where he tried unsuccessfully to reach Bjoernsson.

Meanwhile, the focus of the search shifted to the area north of the camp. While dragging the radar one afternoon, Gordon Scott picked up an unusually

strong reading at a depth of fifty to eighty feet and marked the spot with a blue flag. Spirits were high as everyone began digging a sloping tunnel down to reach whatever was fifty feet below the blue flag. Their heads wrapped in white t-shirts to protect them from the sun, they looked like characters out of a desert adventure movie. But two days later, further radar and magnetometer surveys over the area turned up nothing. After studying the printouts, Bevan announced that Scott's reading was most likely an air pocket marking a buried crevasse.

Toward the end of the second week, with no sign of the planes, the airport at Kulusuk scheduled to close for the weekend and Vaughan unable to reach Bjoernsson, Taylor and Epps reached one of the unspoken decisions that characterized their management style.

"Time's up, right?" Taylor said to Epps.

"Yup," Epps replied. Reluctantly, they shut the expedition down.

BACK IN ATLANTA, EPPS AND TAYLOR IMMEdiately turned their attentions to their neglected businesses. A week later Vaughan came into town and they held a postmortem at the Downwind. There was little cause for optimism. In total, six expeditions had gone to the ice cap in as many years (not counting Epps and Taylor's second, aborted trip in 1981), and it was a matter of conjecture whether anyone had so much as detected objects that *might* be the planes. Having spent approximately $300,000 thus far, Epps and Taylor were financially overextended and the quest seemed more chimerical than ever. To find the aircraft would require larger, betterfunded expeditions, yet given the number of failures, they had little to sell to potential investors. Nonetheless, whenever Epps, Taylor and Vaughan got together, some chemistry took over.

"They were seen less than twenty years ago, so they gotta be there..."

"I'm certain it's the right place, we just haven't found 'em yet..."

"We haven't found them 'cause Bevan's radar wasn't the low-frequency kind..."

"If we'd just had a week or two longer..."

They were unable to raise money for a 1987 expedition. In spring 1988, just when it seemed likely there would be no trip that summer either, Epps attended a banquet in Warner Robins, an agricultural town southeast of Atlanta that was best known as the bedroom community serving Robins Air Force Base. The banquet was to generate interest in expanding an existing aviation museum there, and Epps's father, Ben, was being honored as one of Georgia's aviation pioneers. Since Vaughan was visiting at the time, Epps took him along.

While standing in the buffet line beside a local doctor and his wife, the irrepressible Vaughan began chattering animatedly about lost planes and the Greenland Expedition Society. As he listened, the doctor, Dan Callahan grew intrigued. Soon he was talking to Epps and Taylor about getting involved.

"I'd been cooped up as a medical practitioner for thirty-five years," Callahan would explain later. "Add on about twelve years for education and that's a very long time. I was going to retire soon and I wanted to do something interesting before I got too elderly. My concern was that they were going to say they didn't have enough room in their organization for me."

Room was the only thing the organization had too much of. Epps, who figured a more ambitious expedition would cost upward of $200,000, had come up with a brand-new financing scheme. For $25,000, would-be investors received 4 per cent of the company and a one-eighth share in a P-38. A realist might point out that this really amounted to 4 per cent of a company that was worth nothing and one-eighth of a plane that might not be retrievable or even exist, but Epps and Taylor preferred to focus on the positive. Since a refurbished P-38 had recently sold for $800,000, there was every reason to believe a P-38 from the legendary Lost Squadron could fetch a million. Callahan wrote them a check for $25,000 with the understanding that he'd come along as the expedition's physician.

To Look
Beneath the Ice

THE GEOPHYSICAL TECHNIQUES USED TO LOCATE THE Lost Squadron are essentially the same as those used to find oil, gas or mineral deposits. A transmitter sends out radar waves that gradually diminish in intensity the farther they travel. When the waves strike what is termed an anomaly (any object or feature different from the surrounding area), they are bounced back to the radar's receiver on the surface, similar to the way light reflects from the surface of a mirror.

The ice cap, made up of water, is a relatively easy medium for radio waves to penetrate. For

In dragging a sled back and forth (below), the goal was to record a series of contacts that would pinpoint a plane beneath the surface. This can be done either with fairly simple systems or (as illustrated and below left) more sophisticated models, such as this one featuring separate antennae to transmit and receive signals.

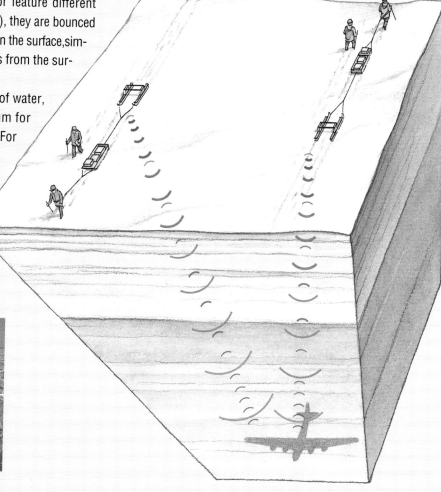

93

the most part, geophysical surveys of the ice cap picked up three kinds of anomalies:

1. Changes in the characteristics of ice at different depths — such as the seventy-foot *firn* line, where granular snow turns into solid glacier ice, or the different layers left by each year's snowfalls. These were easy to identify because they appeared as horizontal lines on the radar's printed profiles.

2. Anomalies within the ice structure. These included pockets of solid ice within the granular snow above the *firn* line, and water pockets in either the *firn* or the solid glacier ice below the *firn* line. In later years, the radar also picked up the metallic debris left by previous expeditions, which could be confusing because it showed up on profiles as a curving arc, which is also how an aircraft would look.

3. The aircraft themselves. The printed profile left by an aircraft at 250 feet turned out to be elongated, like a distinctive rolling hill, as opposed to the steep peak caused by metallic debris closer to the surface.

Using radar to search for the planes was fairly simple. Having established the search area, the radar unit was pulled back and forth across the surface of the ice cap, with the signals radiating outward like ripples in a pond. After picking up a reflection, the geophysicists measured the time it took for the radio waves to reach the object and return. Further readings were taken over a wide area and the object's depth plotted again and again, gradually and methodically homing in on its precise location. At the point at which the radio waves traveled the shortest distance back and forth between the object and the receiver, the operators knew they were directly above a plane.

(Above) A steam probe looses a jet of hot water. Once radar had located a plane, making physical contact was the next step. This was done by pushing a steam probe down through over two hundred feet of ice.

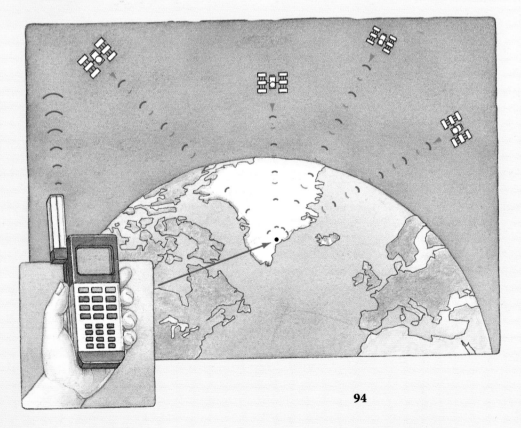

(Left) The final stage once contact had been made would be to determine the aircraft's precise location using the global positioning system. By bouncing a signal off a number of navigation satellites, the GPS unit (inset) would give a plane's precise longitude and latitude.

Most investments, no matter how fanciful, take on momentum once the first investor antes up. Callahan sold the idea to several other doctors, who formed a consortium and contributed another $25,000, and other investors followed. Finally Epps talked to Bobbie Bailey, a dynamic businesswoman active in local cultural affairs. One of four daughters from a dirt-poor family of eight, Bailey had, as a young girl, rebuilt and tuned engines with her older brother. In her twenties she worked for a small machine shop in Atlanta, which she later managed and eventually bought. She built the company, Our-Way, into the world's largest independent rebuilder of commercial air-conditioning and refrigeration compressors while performing charity work, managing local recording artists and getting involved in video and music production on the side. Bailey, who was hardheaded when it came to business, was reluctant at first, then became excited by what she realized was "a great old American story, based right here in Atlanta." In mid-June, the day before the expedition was scheduled to leave, she wrote a check for $12,500 and promised to provide the other half in services.

Of the project's investors, Epps would say, "They're people who can afford to lose $25,000 without going out of business, and there is a chance of finding the airplanes. So what, did we sell them a bill of goods? No, we sold them a piece of a dream." One thing was certain — if the planes weren't located this time, the Greenland Expedition Society wasn't going to be searching for history, it was going to be history.

Epps and Taylor drew up three objectives for the 1988 trip: locate the planes; make contact with a plane to confirm the depth (probably one of the B-17s, since they were the largest targets); and obtain a sample to prove that what they had found was an aircraft. Since Bevan's radar system had failed, they sought alternative expertise.

For several months they had been negotiating with a man named Austin Kovacs, who worked for the Cold Regions Research and Engineering Laboratory (CRREL) in New Hampshire, part of the U.S. Army Corps of Engineers. Although he had trained as a civil engineer, Kovacs's career had taken him into geophysical work in cold climates. At one time he'd worked at radar stations on the DEW line while employed by International Telephone and Telegraph. Later he was stationed at Camp Century, a subterranean research community run by the American government in northeastern Greenland in the early 1960s. Known in the popular press as "the city under the ice," it had a "main street" that was an underground road a quarter of a mile long, and power was provided by an atomic reactor.

Kovacs had been hearing about the Lost Squadron, and by 1988 his interest was piqued. Why, he wondered, had so many expeditions failed to find the planes? After meeting with Epps and Taylor, Kovacs signed on, agreeing to bring subsurface radar and magnetometers, a steam drill to probe for the planes, a mechanical auger system to take a metal sample, and a core barrel to obtain snow-density measurements. He also agreed to supply generators, wooden sleds and other related gear as well as a Global Positioning System (GPS), a navigation devïce that uses satellites to determine latitude and longitude and would record the planes' positions accurately. The total cost, including Kovacs's $20,000 fee, came to nearly $60,000. For their part Epps and Taylor were to provide him with an enclosed all-terrain vehicle to use while operating his radar, cover all travel and accommodation expenses, and ensure there was what Kovacs specified as "good food (not army rations)."

Kovacs would also need help. The name of Bil Thuma, a noted geophysicist from Toronto with whom he had once worked, came to mind.

Thuma was more than a little surprised when Kovacs called him. It had been nearly three years since he'd been to Greenland with the Fiondella-Cox crew, and he'd assumed all the amateur treasure-hunters had given up. Kovacs told him he'd be bringing a radar system and that he wanted Thuma to operate a magnetometer as a backup. Also, Kovacs knew that in 1985 Thuma had used distant peaks as reference points to record accurate positions with a surveyor's transit. That meant he would be able to locate the site on the featureless ice cap. Thuma negotiated a fee of $2,000 from Kovacs.

By early summer, having studied a summary of Helgi Bjoernsson's findings, Kovacs became convinced that the Icelander had found the planes. Epps agreed to send Kovacs to Iceland to evaluate the man's credibility for himself.

Kovacs phoned Epps from Reykjavik.

"I think you should take this guy," he said.

By matching the mountain peaks visible from their camp (below) with those in old photographs (inset), expedition members could narrow down the search area.

96

"What do we need to take him for?" Epps asked. "We've got you — you're our man."

"I've seen his data," Kovacs persisted. "He's qualified and I'm convinced he's found the planes with his radar."

In the end Kovacs convinced Epps to add Bjoernsson to the expedition at GES's expense. Epps agreed, but he and Taylor shook their heads at how complicated the adventure had become. With Kovacs's $60,000 and the Icelanders retained at an additional $25,000, Epps and Taylor had more money tied up in geophysicists than they'd spent on the entire 1986 expedition.

Taylor's biggest headache was finding an enclosed all-terrain vehicle for Kovacs. A snowmobile would do the trick nicely, he thought, but then he discovered that there were no enclosed models. Eventually he found a firm in Buffalo, New York, that manufactured a 750-pound vehicle made of high-density polyethylene with six big bubble tires, a single-cylinder four-stroke engine (built for torque rather than speed) and a detachable canvas top with plastic windows. It cost $6,000 and was too big to be carried in any of the GES planes. Thanks to the efforts of Dan Callahan and an influential supporter at the Smithsonian Institution, however, the air force agreed to carry it in a C-130 Hercules transport on one of its supply trips to Dye 3, the radar station about one hundred miles from the expedition site. To fly it from there directly to the site was prohibitively expensive, so the adventure-loving Taylor enthusiastically proposed that he and Gordon Scott, who

Gordon Scott loads Golf Cart I for the trip to the GES camp on the ice cap. In the background is Dye 3.

Golf Cart I broke its axle on the edge of a crevasse field. Such fissures, often hundreds of feet deep, are hard to see from the ice cap's surface.

had proven so valuable in 1986 that he had been hired as the expedition's technical coordinator, would drive it across the ice cap to the site.

Epps dropped them at Dye 3 on the afternoon of Sunday, June 26. Their first task was to install a pair of tanklike treads, which required repositioning the axles. At midnight, with a light wind blowing and the temperature a comfortable ten below, they finally departed. According to the manufacturer, the vehicle, which was dubbed Golf Cart I, could travel at twenty miles per hour, although Taylor suspected that was at minimum weight along a smooth, downward-sloping asphalt road. At a more realistic ten miles per hour, they could cover one hundred miles in ten hours. But Golf Cart I was heavily loaded with equipment, rolling on treads, not wheels, and traveling across summer *firn* — granular snow on its way to becoming glacier ice. Taylor figured they were going to average five miles per hour, which meant the trip would take about twenty-four hours.

Instead, Golf Cart I traveled at about two miles per hour, which was slightly slower than an average man's walking speed. It also spent a lot of time not traveling at all. Early on Monday morning, an axle broke. It took Taylor and Scott ten hours to remove the treads and wheels, disengage the shifting mechanism and replace the axle. They took turns, one driving the vehicle while the other walked beside it. Every half hour or so they would calculate their direction on a compass, compensating for the deviation of the compass needle east or west of true north

that is caused by the earth's magnetic field. A couple of times, unaware that the other had already adjusted the bearing for deviation, one man would compensate again and Golf Cart I eventually turned forty-five degrees off course. Every time they tried to contact Dye 3 on their radios, all they could raise was static.

They were supposed to arrive at the site on Monday at noon. When they didn't appear by Tuesday afternoon, several expedition members expressed their concern to

Epps. "They're big boys—they can take care of themselves," Epps said. When they didn't appear on Wednesday, both GES planes — the Navajo, based in Kulusuk, and the Cessna 185, piloted by Epps — rendezvoused at Dye 3 and followed the tracks in the snow, which extended straight toward the site, then unexpectedly veered. By the time Epps found the two men, they had broken two more axles and run out of gas on the edge of a dangerous crevasse field. After dropping them fuel and flying the axles to Kulusuk for repairs, Epps guided Golf Cart I from the air, leading the vehicle into camp four days late.

It would make for an entertaining tale at the Downwind, but the Golf Cart I story had been a narrowly averted disaster. During unbuttoned conversations, Taylor could be coaxed into admitting that his and Epps's motto was "Ready, fire, aim." Lighthearted tavern talk, perhaps, but it summed up much of their planning. Although Epps and Taylor were looked upon by most of the amateur crew members as mentors and sages, their inexperience in organizing expeditions to arctic environments was total, and their inclination was to wing it. As a result, the expedition became a circus.

Rather than dropping the geophysicists first to locate the site before bringing in the rest of the equipment and crew, Epps had dropped planeload after planeload of gear. The team of well-intentioned novices ended up with four drop sites spread over an area of more than four square kilometers, and the camp was set up by accident rather than design. Also, they had put the dour Kovacs in charge of the geophysical team, although it soon became apparent that he lacked the diplomatic talents necessary to set up a smooth operation.

The hand-held radios were effective within a radius of only seven miles, and the gray and white tents were difficult to see against the ice cap. The first-aid station consisted of Dan Callahan's black doctor's bag. The food — prepared with more enthusiasm than finesse by the son of an investor — was healthy but didn't begin to replace the 3,000 to 4,000 calories a day or more that each person burned on the ice cap. As Thuma, who was accustomed to working on professional exploration projects sponsored by governments, the military or private industry, said, "Try that at a mining camp in northern Canada and the crew would kill somebody first, then desert."

Using surveying instruments, Thuma took sightings off Refsnoes Mountain to the west, Witch's Tit and Eagle Mountain to the southwest, and Pyramid Peak and Gunsight to the south — the distant peaks visible in 1942 photographs. Having established the coordinates, Thuma and Bjoernsson

Bjoernsson and his crew confer during their systematic search for an aircraft.

adjusted them to take into account the glacier's estimated drift, which placed their search parameters nearly a mile southeast of the 1942 site. Then Bjoernsson, Jon Sveinsson and Addi Hermannsson began running the low-frequency radar.

Thuma, meanwhile, was frustrated. His magnetometer had arrived late and then wouldn't work because the area was littered with steel pipes, generators and other metal gear dropped by the over-eager Epps. Although he liked and admired Epps and Taylor for their drive and energy, he was shocked by the Boy Scout character of the expedition. He wrote in his journal, "No unifying force...no leader, no defined objectives, no focus." Unable to do his job, he helped the Icelanders.

In the end, any credit for the expedition's success went to Bjoernsson. As an admiring Taylor put it, Bjoernsson was "a bona fide, sho'nuff European-style professor's professor." Every day he ignored the confusion in the camp around him and concentrated on his mission. Bjoernsson's faith was science, and his Icescope a testament to ingenuity. The homemade equipment was pulled behind Golf Cart I in a grid pattern. A couple of times a day, Bjoernsson, Sveinsson and Hermannsson huddled in their tent studying the developed film. Finally, on Thursday, June 30, the Icescope located a large object — large enough to be a B-17 bomber — more than two hundred feet under the ice.

Over the next few days, various crew members took turns lowering Kovacs's steam probe through the ice, hoping to bump against something at the depth indicated by Bjoernsson's radar. It was an ingenious system. A homemade solar collector melted ice and snow, which filled a plastic-lined reservoir a little larger than a child's wading pool. ("Solar radiation produces 400 BTUs per square foot per hour," Taylor explained. "So twenty-four hours of sunlight melts a lot of snow.") Water from the pool was heated in a generator-powered boiler and pumped through three hundred feet of high-pressure hose to a brass nozzle. Warm runoff water from the boiler was bled back into the pool.

(Below left) Golf Cart I pulling Bjoernsson's radar. **(Below right)** Once an aircraft was detected, the next step was to try to touch it with a steam probe pushed down through the ice.

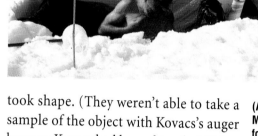

One day, after more than a week on the ice cap without a bath, Kovacs felt the water and impulsively removed his clothing.

"Hey," he yelled to Taylor and a few others who were working nearby. They stared in astonishment at the naked figure standing in the snow.

"Come on over—the water's fine." Then he stepped into the reservoir and sat down. Soon everyone was lined up for their turn in the ice-cap bathtub.

Operating the steam probe was laborious work. To travel straight down, the nozzle couldn't actually touch the ice. That meant the hose had to be draped over a man's shoulders while he supported its weight. Time after time the entire three hundred feet was played out, then hauled to the surface to begin again.

At 10:30 P.M. on Saturday, July 2, Thuma was operating the probe when he made contact with something at 250 feet. Two more contacts were made that night within a radius of ten feet. Two days later, having marked several more hits with flags, the approximate outline of an airplane wing took shape. (They weren't able to take a sample of the object with Kovacs's auger because Kovacs had brought only 165 feet of extension pipe.)

The Icelanders, using the first site as a reference point, located seven more objects with the Icescope. With mounting excitement, Epps and Taylor compared the Icelanders' markers with the configuration of the squadron. They matched. "They might not be planes," Taylor pointed out, sounding uncharacteristically cautious. "They might be behemoths, for all we know. But if so, the behemoths died in a pattern that corresponds to how the planes landed in '42."

Epps, Taylor and Vaughan spent time comparing notes and studying the 1942 photographs. They identified each plane, including the one they'd hit with the probe, and, using their Global Positioning System, fixed the latitude and longitude of their positions. By then, Taylor's customary optimism had returned.

"Gentlemen," said Taylor. "Here lies *Big Stoop*."

(Above left) Melting snow for the boiler. (Right) Richard Taylor takes a bath in the meltwater.

ON MONDAY, JULY 4, INDEPENDENCE DAY, the crew assembled at the site of *Big Stoop*. Taylor, wearing a blue ski jacket and trousers, took off his navy blue tuque and recited the Twenty-third Psalm. Then, looking around the ice cap, he solemnly said, "This is the Lord's House in its purest form, and I'm proud to be here and I'm proud to be involved in this great project." It was an emotional moment, with everyone shaking hands and bear-hugging.

Four days later a helicopter from Kulusuk arrived to fly out the geophysicists and their equipment as well as most of the crew. Norman Vaughan, Gordon Scott and Chiel "C. W." Marlow, a former bank executive and air force pilot who was GES's executive director at the time, stayed behind to begin work on a tunnel. A tunnel dug on a thirty-degree slope had first been conceived of as a way to reach planes that were eighty feet deep. Even though the planes were 250 feet deep, Epps and Taylor felt that valuable information about excavating ice and snow could be gained by going ahead with the digging. Besides, a return helicopter flight would cost several thousand dollars. Epps, who was catching a commercial flight home that day, assured them that Neil Estes, a motorcycle-racing buddy of Taylor's who was a pilot and skilled mechanic, was arriving from Atlanta late that afternoon and would fly the Cessna back to the site. Vaughan, Scott and Marlow began digging, first with shovels and later with a pair of chain saws.

Thursday and Friday passed without sign of Estes. The digging party knew the Kulusuk airport was closed for the weekend, and although they had plenty of food they stopped using the chain saws on Sunday because they were running low on fuel. On Monday afternoon, when there was still no sign of the plane, Marlow looked at his watch and said, "Well, Pat and Richard are sitting in the Rotary Club right now, enjoying a nice meal in a warm room, and they don't even know we're here." He was being flip, but Marlow was unnerved. They had estimated that in the event of an emergency, it would take Scott five days to reach Angmagssalik on foot. In his diary Marlow wrote, "We, all of us, really feel abandoned. We have been here five days, no communications, low on fuel, and nothing to do."

On Wednesday, Marlow spotted a distant plane's contrail. Tuning into the emergency frequency on one of the hand-held radios, he said, "Airplane approaching southeast coast of Greenland. Can you read us?" When the pilot answered, Marlow explained who they were and asked him to contact Kulusuk to see whether anyone was coming out to the camp. The pilot reported that someone had been trying but at present all flights were grounded due to heavy cloud.

Finally on Saturday, after ten days on the ice cap, Marlow, Vaughan and Scott heard the drone of the Cessna's engine and directed Estes to the camp by radio. Then Estes got out and Marlow piloted the plane back to Kulusuk. When he arrived, he phoned Taylor and told him to wire funds to hire a helicopter to airlift the remaining men and equipment off the ice cap. It could have turned tragic; instead, it was another tale destined to be repeated and embellished at

A helicopter took out most of the expedition members. After it left, Vaughan and two others found themselves stranded on the ice for several days.

the Downwind, another example of the extraordinary good luck that blessed the Greenland Expedition Society.

Back in Atlanta Epps and Taylor found themselves the center of media attention. In keeping with their personalities and the spirit of the endeavor, both men became masters of hyperbole, spinning stories the journalists rarely questioned. Taylor told an Associated Press reporter that GES planned to construct a tunnel to the planes, "then, if we can, Pat Epps and I are going to fly two of them off the ice." Epps and Taylor knew that excavating the aircraft at 250 feet was going to require a massive engineering program. And, as Brad McManus

could testify, landing or taking off on the ice cap in a P-38 was dangerous, probably impossible. Especially in a plane that had spent forty years locked in a glacier.

But pragmatism was for private planning sessions; Epps and Taylor did their dreaming in public. When an Italian film crew visited Atlanta, the two men performed like a vaudeville team in front of the Cessna at DeKalb-Peachtree Airport.

"We'll clean the airplane up..." said Epps.

"...add fuel," interjected Taylor.

"...run the engines up..." continued Epps.

"...put in a new battery..."

"...point it down the runway and off across the snowfield we'll go."

PART THREE

THE RECOVERY

CHAPTER FOUR

TAR BABY

I N "TAR BABY," ONE OF THE BEST-KNOWN stories by the nineteenth-century southern author Joel Chandler Harris, Br'er Rabbit finds a tar doll by the side of the road. Angered when it won't answer him, he hits it. When his paw sticks, he hits with the other paw, then with both rear legs, until he's stuck tight.

In September 1988, Pat Epps sat in his office overlooking the runway at DeKalb-Peachtree Airport, feeling like Br'er Rabbit as he pondered his obsession with the Lost Squadron. Struggling to put his thoughts into words years later, he said, "You gotta go back in '89. Why? Damned if I know. You get a reading with the radar. You touch it with the steam probe. Is it really an airplane? Your curiosity has got you so you gotta go back. It's like the Tar Baby."

At about the same time, in Douglas, a small city in the sun-baked Georgia flatlands about two hundred miles south of Atlanta, Don Brooks was dialing Epps's phone number. Brooks, who had been following the search for the Lost Squadron

for several years, had read an article in the *Atlanta Journal-Constitution* about how Epps and Taylor had touched one of the eight planes and were making plans to excavate them all the following summer. Brooks thought it sounded like the kind of great adventure that was getting harder and harder to find in the modern world. Furthermore, it was wonderful that a pair of southern boys were doing it on a shoestring budget, relying on old-fashioned initiative and know-how. Brooks, who loved aviation history, believed that recovering historic aircraft so future generations could see them was a worthwhile cause. But what really caught his interest was the fact that two of the planes were B-17 bombers.

Brooks had been very close to his father, who had trained as a pilot but served in World War II as a B-17 tail-gunner, surviving without injury while scores of his companions were maimed or killed. After the war, Brooks's father didn't pursue flying ("Muh daddy always said he felt like he'd used up all his luck with airplanes"), but he encouraged his son to get his pilot's license, promising him that when he did, he'd join him as a passenger. His father died in 1978, shortly before Brooks received his license. On the day Brooks soloed he was consumed

not only by the exhilarating high of piloting a plane alone but by the thought that his father had experienced the same feelings decades earlier. Now the Greenland Expedition Society offered an opportunity to fulfill one of his fondest dreams: to restore a B-17, paint it in the colors of his father's 390th bomber group, and fly it at air shows.

Although he had never met Epps, Brooks used DeKalb-Peachtree Airport whenever he flew his small plane into Atlanta and had, coincidentally, been doing business at Epps Aviation for years. When Epps answered his phone, Brooks introduced himself, his south Georgia accent as thick as syrup. "I hear y'all found a B-17," he said. "Muh daddy was a gunner in a B-17 and I want one. I'd like to be a member of your group."

Epps, thinking fast, outlined the conditions. Before the June expedition, he explained, investors paid $25,000 per share even though there was no guarantee that the planes could be found. Then, he continued, we located them with the radar and thumped down on one, and they're only *eighty meters deep.* (Epps always referred to the planes' depth in metric, since eighty meters sounded less daunting than 250 feet.) Epps told Brooks that GES was putting together an engineering program to recover the planes (failing to mention that the program existed mainly as an engineering theory rather than anything solid.)

"So, Mr. Brooks," Epps concluded, "in fairness to our other investors, we feel we'll have to charge you a little more. We believe a share is now worth $75,000."

Brooks said he would like to think about it. He called Epps the following day.

"I don't deny that what you're askin' is a fair price," Brooks said, "but y'all askin' me to pay three times what your original investors paid. When they put in $25,000, the planes were only forty feet deep. Now the planes are two hun'ert and fifty feet deep, so I'm only willing to pay twice as much. If y'all want to accept a check for $50,000, you can."

Since no one else was offering so much as fifty cents, Epps and Taylor quickly accepted and Brooks became a member of GES. He also became a good friend and a counterbalance to their leadership. Where Epps and Taylor were, each in his own way, wildly optimistic and driven by a kind of frantic urgency, the soft-spoken Brooks was methodical and thorough. A stocky thirty-eight-year-old with alert gray eyes, he was utterly without pretense and possessed a wry good-ol'-boy sense of humor. At one of their early meetings, Taylor inquired about his work.

"Ah got a parts store," Brooks said.

"How did you get into that business?" Taylor asked.

"Whall," Brooks said, "muh daddy had a parts store."

"Must be a good business down there."

"Yup."

"Is it a big store?"

"Whall," Brooks said, smiling. "It's a coupla stores."

"How many is a couple?" Taylor asked.

"Fifty."

Taylor laughed. "Fifty? That's huge, isn't it? How many people in south Georgia got more than that?"

"I dunno," said Brooks, his eyes twinkling. "Maybe nobody."

(continued on page 115)

(Above) A B-17 Flying Fortress bombs a German airfield in France, in 1944.

(Below) B-17s flying in the tight formation used by American bomber crews to carry out pinpoint daylight bombing. The vapor trails above them are from their fighter escorts.

(Overleaf) Flying Fortresses could withstand punishing damage. This painting by William Phillips depicts a B-17, with one engine knocked out, limping home to England escorted by two P-47s.

The Flying Fortress

IF ONE AIRCRAFT HAD TO BE CHOSEN TO SYMBOLIZE the Allied effort during World War II, it would be the legendary B-17 Flying Fortress. The first four-engine bomber, it was the only front-line U.S. combat aircraft in continual use throughout the war. Although its contemporary, the B-24 Liberator, was produced in greater numbers and carried a larger bomb load, it was the B-17 that spearheaded the U.S. bombing offensive in Europe as well as being used extensively in the Mediterranean and Pacific theaters. Pilots and crew loved it: its top speed equaled that of most single-engine fighters and its rugged construction was able to absorb an enormous amount of damage.

(continued on page 113)

Many veterans tell stories of B-17s with gaping holes in the fuselage and part of a wing torn off flying home on one or two engines.

The B-17 represented a perfect marriage of technology and timing. By the mid-1930s, Boeing was already considered a progressive firm that had pioneered many aerodynamic features on earlier state-of-the-art planes. In 1934, when the Army Air Corps invited the major aircraft companies to design a multiengine bomber, Boeing responded with what was at the time a revolutionary proposal. While most long-range bombers of the period were powered by two engines, Boeing's team, spearheaded by Edward C. Wells, the company's young engineering genius, came up with a four-engine design. The prototype made its maiden flight in 1935, flying two thousand miles non-stop at unprecedented altitudes and speeds. The aircraft so impressed one newspaper reporter that he described it as a "veritable flying fortress." Boeing later registered the name as an official trademark, although ground and air crews invariably called it the "17."

By 1937, the addition of turbosupercharged engines meant that the first B-17s to roll off the production line could fly at 30,000 feet, which put them out of reach of any antiaircraft weapons then in use. Two years later, with war declared in Europe, Britain's Royal Air Force began using B-17s. Weaknesses emerged that might have scuttled further production of the plane — it was vulnerable to attack from the front and rear and its guns tended to freeze at high altitudes — but Boeing refined the aircraft through a total of seven models, adding self-sealing gas tanks and protective armor, improving defensive armament and increasing

Airborne for the first time in 1935, the B-17 was the first modern four-engine bomber.

the size of its flying surfaces to provide greater stability for bombing.

B-17s were critical to the American strategy of daylight bombing raids against Nazi airfields, oil depots, power stations, factories and other targets. Its superiority lay in its ability to fly at high altitudes in tight formations of a dozen or more planes; an armada of Flying Fortresses was less vulnerable to attack by enemy fighters and produced superior bomb patterns. But pinpoint bombing required meticulous control, and B-17s were equipped with one of the Allied forces' most secret weapons: a highly accurate optical instrument called the Norden bombsight.

By 1941, when the Norden was connected to a gyrostabilized automatic-pilot system, it could instantly and precisely compute bomb trajectories while taking into account the plane's speed, altitude and drift. The Norden

had a reputation for being able to "drop a bomb in a pickle barrel" from twenty thousand feet, although that kind of precision was only possible when the aircraft was flying on a straight, level course over clear skies, conditions rarely found over industrial targets in wartime Germany. Adding to the mystique was the way armed guards installed the carefully shrouded bombsight in a B-17 shortly before takeoff and removed it immediately after landing. In the event that an aircraft was forced down, pilots were to destroy the Norden rather than let it get into enemy hands.

No combat plane contributed more to the success of the Allied forces in Europe. Major General Carl "Tooey" Spaatz, whose Eighth Air Force was responsible for mounting the airborne offensive against the Nazis, once said that World War II could not have been won without the B-17.

Brooks was exactly the kind of committed participant GES needed. He wanted to contribute in a substantial way to the operation, so he began learning everything he could about the ice cap and previous expeditions. Since he had a technical bent, he consulted frequently with Gil Lund, project manager for Seattle-based Hamilton Engineering Inc., a company specializing in geophysical exploration that was interested in retrieving the aircraft. At GES's expense, Lund had drawn up a proposal, which Brooks studied in detail.

Lund proposed excavating a ten-foot-diameter shaft to each plane, with the excavated ice removed from the site by a pneumatic blowing system used in the mining industry. The shaft would be kept narrow to minimize the amount of snow and ice they'd have to remove. After hollowing out a cavern around the planes, mechanics would dismantle them and each section would be hauled to the surface by winches. The cost was estimated to be at least $1.5 million. Although many newspaper accounts referred to Epps and Taylor as "two wealthy Atlanta-based adventurers," everyone associated with the project, including Lund, knew that the program would only go ahead if GES secured a major source of financing.

Although the period of limitless deal-making and sky-high financing that characterized U.S. business during the mid-1980s had not yet wound down, GES wasn't close to raising the kind of funds necessary to underwrite Lund's project. Epps and Taylor were trying to secure sponsorship with what they described in GES's

annual report as "a patriotic corporation with an interest in aviation history [which] would bear a substantial amount of the financial responsibility in exchange for world-wide media exposure and a sense of tremendous historical achievement."

There were no takers. It was simply too small, too provincial, too speculative, too peculiar an endeavor to interest most investors, especially at a time when major corporations were preoccupied with protecting themselves against (or engineering) hostile takeovers. Once again the 1989 expedition was left to imaginative amateurs like Epps, Taylor and Brooks, who brainstormed solutions in their Downwind think tank, constructed them on home workbenches and financed them on a wing and a prayer.

Since GES's agreement with the Danish government was due to expire that year, the primary goal was to produce "tangible evidence" of the aircraft. If that was successful, the next phase of the expedition would begin: digging down to a plane to examine it and, if possible, remove it. If the 1989 expedition failed, prospects were gloomy. As Epps told the *Boston Globe*, "If we don't produce a piece of the airplane this time, we would have to retire from the effort."

Taylor had an idea. First he went to a hardware store and bought a carpenter's mortise drill, a tool that removes waste wood while boring a hole. Then he drove to the warehouse where Patrick Epps, Jr., ran a business buying and selling wrecked airplane parts. When Taylor tried boring holes into airplane wings and fuselages, he was excited to see that a small quantity of metal was extracted by the drill. The principle worked. He then met Bobbie Bailey, who commissioned her engineering staff at Our-Way to design a coring device consisting of a drill, equipped with flanges, that could extract a piece of metal from a plane.

In the meantime Brooks took it upon himself to finance the expedition, which would eventually cost more than $300,000. He assembled the equipment and supplies and, since he loved any kind of mechanical or engineering puzzle, he spent countless hours thinking about inexpensive ways of tunneling to the planes. He performed endless calculations, factoring in such variables as the likely maximum number of days of good weather on the ice cap and the amount and speed at which various kinds of equipment could move snow. Researchers at Georgia Tech suggested using a plasma arc torch — a tool for cutting steel and other hard materials, using compressed air and high-voltage electricity. That seemed highly speculative and costly. Other ideas were wildly imaginative or simply outlandish. Someone at the Downwind suggested pointing the back end of a jet engine toward the ice and letting the blast of hot exhaust gases melt the hole.

In addition to his auto-parts chain, Brooks owned a company that built hot-water pressure washers. Working there, he devised a steamer that would melt a three-foot-diameter shaft through the ice cap. His prototype had copper coils wrapped around its nose through which hot water would be pumped. Epps and Taylor were excited by this simple and inexpensive method of reaching a plane, so Brooks decided to run it by Gil Lund.

Even though it was obvious that GES wasn't going to raise the financing necessary to carry out his proposal, Lund was so intrigued by the project that he remained involved. He flew to Douglas to help Brooks fine-tune the design, and at his suggestion Brooks rebuilt the device with a stainless-steel cone. Since everyone believed that the hole might ice up behind the steamer, Brooks outfitted the tail with a "reverse taper" containing twenty-four nozzles that sprayed hot water like a fountain. It had two purposes. If the steamer successfully sank a shaft to the tunnel, the fountain would melt a small cavern around that area of the plane; if ice began to build up inside the hole, the fountain would help the steamer melt its way back up. Brooks called his invention a "thermal meltdown generator."

Coring equipment, meltdown generators and the crews to run them meant transportation was becoming a serious problem — more than a ski-equipped Cessna could handle. To Epps, Taylor and Brooks the solution sat on the tarmac next door to Epps Aviation. It was a DC-3 — a rugged twin-engine plane that was equally effective carrying passengers or cargo. The aircraft in question had been used during World War II and was eventually purchased by a firm that flew out of DeKalb-Peachtree. It was for sale and, upon investigation, proved to have been beautifully reconditioned, with every control and cable replaced and new wings installed. At first Epps and Taylor thought GES might buy it, but the $175,000 price

Although designed as passenger liners, thousands of DC-3s served in the American forces during World War II as the C-47 Skytrain and in the British and Commonwealth air forces as the Dakota. Don Brooks's DC-3 had been built in 1944 and transferred from the United States Army Air Corps to Britain's Royal Air Force in time to take part in the Normandy invasion. Brooks's plane also participated in the airborne crossing of the Rhine in 1945. After the war it went to Canada, and served as a navigation trainer with the Royal Canadian Air Force. In 1970 the plane was sold to a civilian buyer, ending an eventful military career with three different air forces that had spanned a quarter of a century.

was too steep. Then Brooks, who wanted to be an active player and felt that others had been contributing for several years before him, offered to chip in but it was still too much. Finally Brooks told them that since they had been bearing the burden of the project for years, he would buy the plane and lease it back to GES: "When we dig up the Lost Squadron and the money comes in, we'll settle up."

Brooks enlisted his friend Bob Harless to pilot and maintain the DC-3. Harless had been a director of maintenance for Southern Airways when its main aircraft were DC-3s, and he later piloted one. He managed the airfield in Douglas where

Brooks kept his plane, and he needed little coaxing to take over the care and flying of a DC-3 involved in so remarkable a venture.

Their biggest problem was finding skis. They finally located a set and Harless, at Brooks's expense, drove from Douglas to Yellowknife, in Canada's Northwest Territories, to purchase them. Brooks had only been involved in the search for the Lost Squadron for six months, and already he'd acquired a veteran's sense of irony. As he would later observe, "They drove futhah from Dh'uglas to Yellaknife to get skis than we flew from Dh'uglas to Greenland and back."

THE 1989 EXPEDITION WAS SCHEDULED TO leave Atlanta on Friday, July 7, at 8:30 A.M. GES had hired a public-relations specialist to work on their behalf, and he was responsible for the TV crews from local ABC, CBS and NBC outlets and CNN as well as a few newspaper reporters who gathered on the tarmac at DeKalb-Peachtree Airport to interview Epps and Taylor and record the departure. At 10:00 A.M. the engines started. Then a mechanical problem in the tail assembly had to be repaired. Shortly before noon, as Epps tried to start the plane, a mag switch broke. Without it one of the two engines could not be started. The switch was common to several different 1940s vintage aircraft, but how long would it take to find one? Fortunately, Epps's brother, Ben, a former World War II pilot and noted pack rat, had come by to witness the departure. "I think I've got one of those in my garage," he said. Finally, at 1:30 P.M., the Greenland Expedition Society took off.

Three days later the DC-3 dropped its load of gear and most of its passengers at Kulusuk. Brooks, Norman Vaughan and Doug Epps continued on to Reykjavik, where five thousand pounds of equipment — including Brooks's "thermal meltdown generator" — had been shipped in advance by air freight. In the Cessna, Epps flew Taylor and an advance party of five to the ice cap to establish the camp.

Conditions were balmy — fifty-seven degrees Fahrenheit under clear skies — but a stiff forty mile-per-hour wind reminded Taylor that in Greenland, the highest authority was the weather. At the end of the previous year's expedition, Addi Hermannsson, who had assisted Helgi Bjoernsson with his Icescope, had left electronic markers used for ski patrolling at each plane. After digging in their tents, Taylor and Hermannsson tried to pick up signals with a remote sensor, but the markers had either blown away or malfunctioned. Epps returned to fly Hermannsson back to Kulusuk where he contacted his colleague, Jon Sveinsson, in Reykjavik. Sveinsson agreed to bring the Icescope by Monday.

"Spirits are running high even though we have setbacks," Taylor wrote in his journal that night. "Sunburn seems to be our only problem...noses and cheeks fry from the direct sun and reflection off the snow. We're looking for the DC-3 anytime now to bring fresh supplies."

The DC-3, however, was grounded indefinitely in Reykjavik due to bad weather, and fog on the ice cap prevented Epps from flying back in from Kulusuk. The fog lasted for several days, punctuated by light rain or snow. By the weekend their food supplies consisted of some freeze-dried chicken teriyaki, macaroni, baked beans, two cans of tuna, cereal, coffee and hot chocolate, M&Ms, raisins and canned peanuts. There was no fuel for cooking or heat. By Sunday Taylor had restricted the camp to one meal per day. Without a generator to recharge the batteries, he could only use the radio to contact Kulusuk sparingly. And without the Icescope, there was little to do but lie around in sleeping bags reading, swapping explorer stories or playing hearts, a game at which Gordon Scott excelled. For exercise they played Frisbee in the fog.

After several delays caused by bad weather and minor breakdowns, the DC-3 finally landed on the ice cap. Expedition members then unloaded gear, including the large boiler needed to heat water for the steam probes.

At noon on Wednesday, July 19, the DC-3 made it into Kulusuk with the expedition's supplies. The next day Epps flew the Cessna through a light overcast to drop off Sveinsson and the Icescope. The weather and minor repairs prevented the DC-3 from leaving Kulusuk, so he returned several times with food, equipment and passengers. Soon the population on the ice cap included Doug Epps and Norman Vaughan; Brooks and Harless; Fafnir "Iceman" Frostason, a young Icelandic pilot who was upgrading his license at Epps Aviation when Epps engaged him to fly the Cessna; and

Gil Lund, whose expenses had been paid but who was donating his time to be part of the expedition. Also present were Lou Sapienza, a professional photographer, and a three-man documentary film crew from Vancouver, all of whom good-naturedly performed their share of camp duties in addition to recording events.

By midnight Sveinsson had located *Big Stoop*, and on Friday Taylor, Neil Estes and Gordon Scott began lowering the steam probe. The steam probe, similar in principle to the one Austin Kovacs had used the previous year, had been built by Don

Brooks. It consisted of a converted automobile engine steam cleaner coupled to three hundred feet of high-pressure hose that ended in an eight-foot pipe with a nozzle tip. Water was drawn from two large solar collectors and power was supplied by two 6,500-watt gasoline-powered generators.

The first three holes were misses. Retrieving the hose was back-breaking labor, the equivalent of hauling it up a twenty-five-story building. Although everyone worked hard, the indefatigable Scott shouldered the bulk of the task, drawing up the hose as casually as if he were pulling line from an ice-fishing hole.

On Saturday it rained so heavily that work was delayed until midafternoon. On the fourth hole, Scott felt the hose vibrate briefly at about the 250-foot mark, then continue to descend. A strike, but a glancing one. Finally, on the morning of Tuesday, July 25, as Scott and Estes steamed the eighth hole, they scored a solid hit that scarred the tip of the probe.

That was cause for celebration at the tiny tent city on the ice cap. For years the weather and the ice cap had worked together to form an unbeatable opponent. Suddenly, in their fifth matchup and despite heavy rain, the GES team was moving into the lead.

On Wednesday a bigger head was mounted on the probe to enlarge the hole. The crew assembled the tripod and drilling rig supplied by Bobbie Bailey's Our-Way, and began coupling together twenty-five

To recover a piece of Big Stoop from more than 250 feet below the surface, members of the GES constructed the world's longest hand drill (left and middle), a special bit attached to many joined sections of aluminum pipe. Then the drill was driven into the plane (right).

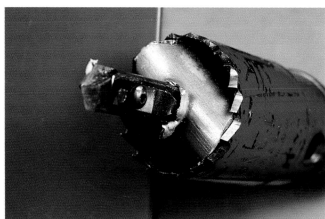

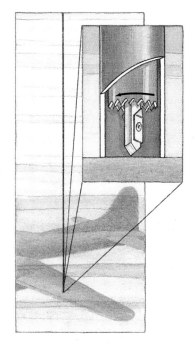

(Above) Pat Epps works the drill bit loose from the aluminum pipe. (Top right) Proof positive. A piece of Big Stoop had lodged in the drill, which (bottom right) had successfully cut away a tiny piece of the plane.

ten-foot sections of 2½-inch PVC pipe and lowering them, piece by piece, down the hole. These would act as the sleeve to guide the coring device. After pouring hot water into the pipe to melt any ice that may have formed, they inserted a ten-foot-long, ¾-inch aluminum tube that held Bailey's drill bit. Then they threaded together twenty-four additional sections of tubing and fed them down the hole. Forty-five minutes later, they had constructed a 250-foot-long hand-drill.

They turned the crank. Nothing. No one had remembered that each ten-foot section needed to be tightened with a wrench. With Norman Vaughan supervising the sorting and stacking of pipes and couplings, they pulled the tubes out and then put them back, this time tightening each section.

Epps turned the crank. There was a distinct *thunk* and the drill dropped an inch. Pay dirt! The crew hauled the drill to the surface. Embedded inside the coring device was a piece of aluminum tubing about

½-inch in diameter.

Ragged cheers carried across the ice cap. Neil Estes opened a magnum of Moët & Chandon Brut Imperial. The filmmakers filmed and Sapienza snapped pictures. Taylor held up a portable tape recorder and announced that Bobbie Bailey had given him a tape to play when a piece of the plane was removed. He punched play and Diana Ross sang "The Impossible Dream."

With tangible evidence of the aircraft in hand and five days remaining on the ice cap, Epps and Taylor agreed to begin the second phase of the expedition. Brooks's thermal meltdown generator, which resembled a torpedo with a giant stainless-steel nose cone, was suspended by chains over the B-17's location. Water from the solar

(Above) In the background behind Pat Epps, the frame for the thermal meltdown generator is erected. (Right) Running night and day, this device could melt a hole at two feet an hour.

collector fed into the generator-powered boiler, and hot water was pumped into the meltdown device. By keeping the hot nose cone just above the ice, it would, in theory, melt straight down as it was lowered.

It was a slow process: the rate of descent was about two feet per hour. And for the operator it was a delicate process. If the nose cone rested on the ice, the meltdown generator tipped over and veered off-course. Once it melted down far enough to be out of sight, it grew increasingly difficult to judge how quickly to lower it. Several times it began to burrow sideways but was righted. (Taylor, who noted that the hero of Robert Ballard's search for the shipwrecked *Titanic* was a remote-controlled undersea video robot named Jason, dubbed Brooks's invention the Gopher.) One phenomenon was duly noted. The warmth rising up the shaft behind the meltdown generator enlarged its diameter. They wouldn't be needing the reverse taper.

Gil Lund was on the night shift when the Gopher veered off-course at seventy feet. Since the expedition was nearly over, he

(Above) The thermal meltdown generator had to be watched constantly to prevent the cone from touching the ice, which would cause it to veer off sideways. (Right) After the 1989 expedition, the GES made it into Ripley's Believe It or Not!

slackened the chain to see what it would do. It turned over and jammed itself sideways into the ice. Scott donned climbing gear and rappelled down the three-foot-wide hole, managing to work the Gopher free so it could be pulled to the surface.

Epps, Taylor and Brooks evaluated the operation. The boiler was working, but the generator powering it had failed. The supply of water from the solar collector was inadequate and the PVC pipes feeding hot water to the Gopher were distorting from the heat. Meanwhile, at the neighboring drill site, subsequent corings extracted a quantity of ice saturated with what appeared to be engine oil and a piece of metal to which a nut and a fragment of a bolt were attached. They speculated that the second piece, which was flat and a drab olive green, the color of a World War II B-17, was probably from the skin of the plane. Best of all, neither of the metal fragments appeared to be crushed.

It was the end of the month and many of the key crew members had business and family responsibilities that needed their

attention. On Saturday, July 29, they struck camp, and the DC-3 and Cessna flew in to start moving people and equipment off the ice.

When Epps and Taylor returned to Atlanta, they were besieged with requests for interviews. The story was carried throughout the U.S. and abroad on TV, radio and in newspapers. The media loved the Georgia-crackers-on-an-adventure aspect of the project, and Epps and Taylor could be counted on for some folksy quotes. (In one Associated Press article that ran in dozens of papers, Epps told the reporter, "We dropped our fishing pole down and brought back a piece of the airplane we'd been looking for for eight years.")

At the end of the year, a sign that they had really arrived appeared in hundreds of weekend newspapers. The internationally syndicated *Ripley's Believe It or Not* featured the discovery of the Lost Squadron alongside an item on the longest recorded distance for gum-boot tossing.

IN EARLY 1990, HAVING WON AN EXTENSION on their salvage rights by producing tangible evidence of the planes, Epps and Taylor faced the perennial problem of raising money to keep GES alive. They contacted B. F. Goodrich, which had made small but welcome contributions in the past, to see whether the company would take a more substantial position in 1990. It declined. They contacted Boeing and Lockheed again and made a pitch to McDonnell-Douglas, the aerospace firm that had manufactured Brooks's DC-3 half a century earlier. They made a presentation to the Georgia Department of Industry and Trade, hoping to attract a consortium of corporate investors. Taylor even went through an issue of *National Geographic,* writing down the names of every corporation that had bought more than a half-page ad, then wrote letters to all the companies on the list, which included Toyota, Ford and Rolex. In what was becoming an annual ritual, no one was interested.

A less formal approach proved more successful. Months earlier, Epps had run an ad in *Trade-A-Plane,* a used-aircraft publication: "For Sale. Lockheed P-38F Lightning. 50 hours total time. $259,000." (Epps wanted $250,000 for the plane, so he tacked on $9,000 to allow a prospective buyer to talk him down.) Below, in smaller print, the text read, "To help fund this expedition, the G.E.S. offers one of the aircraft as is, where is."

Among many curious callers were several wealthy aviation enthusiasts who sniffed around the project but didn't commit, and one who did. Dr. Wes Stricker was an allergy and asthma specialist from Missouri who operated a chain of clinics and research labs. For $100,000, Stricker, a pilot who owned several historic aircraft, purchased the right of first refusal on the third airplane to be recovered, with the understanding that he would examine the plane under the ice and decide whether it was

salvageable. If so, he could buy the plane outright by kicking in the remaining $159,000. But even with Stricker's participation, Epps and Taylor estimated they'd need at least another $750,000.

Around Thanksgiving weekend, Epps was visiting relatives in Seattle when someone recommended that he contact a Vermont-based contractor named Angelo Pizzagalli. Coincidentally, one of Epps's brothers had had agreeable business dealings with Pizzagalli Construction. Over the next few months, Epps, Taylor and Brooks made several trips to Burlington, Vermont, to talk to Pizzagalli, who turned out to be excited by the project and willing to finance the excavation of a plane.

Epps and Brooks were delighted. The Pizzagalli brothers — Angelo and Remo — were general contractors specializing in sewage treatment plants. That meant they

The ad that Pat Epps placed in Trade-A-Plane to drum up investors in the GES's 1990 expedition. By offering a P-38 at the low price of $259,000, Epps hoped to find an investor who might not be daunted by the plane's location.

were experienced at digging deep excavations and dealing with water and, by virtue of their location, working in cold weather. They'd also built power plants and dams and had worked in remote locations in the Caribbean. Furthermore, their company had a reputation for being innovative. Years earlier, for example, while laying pipeline into a lake, they'd discovered that the lake bottom was solid rock. To solve the problem, they'd modified their drilling equipment so they could drive their gear into the water. Although underwater construction has since become common, the Pizzagallis were among the first to experiment with it.

Slowly they began to firm up details for a cooperative expedition that would take place in the summer of 1990. With Angelo in charge, the Pizzagalli brothers, who were underwriting the project personally and had created a company called ROLLS Ltd. to that end, would be responsible for supplying all of the technology and equipment necessary to sink a shaft to a P-38 and remove it. GES was to handle all the logistics: locating the planes, establishing and maintaining the camp, supplying food, fuel and related support materials, and providing all transportation to and from the ice cap. The main restriction was that Angelo Pizzagalli's cargo had to fit into the DC-3.

To Epps and Brooks, the deal drew upon GES's experience living and working on the ice cap while relieving it of the part of the project with which they were least experienced. As Brooks remarked on one of their flights back to Atlanta, "Having Pizzagalli involved is the best thing that's happened to the Greenland Expedition Society."

Taylor wasn't so sure. Although he liked Angelo Pizzagalli — they shared a professional interest in design and engineering and a personal interest in car racing — he grew increasingly skeptical of his approach.

Pizzagalli's plan was to use a modified silo unloader equipped with steel blades to cut a shaft sixteen feet in diameter to the plane. The technology made sense — in cold climates, grain at the top of silos is usually frozen, and silo unloaders efficiently chew it up — but all the equipment was going to be more than the DC-3 could carry. So Epps worked his network of aviation contacts and eventually persuaded the Air Force to let him lease a couple of C-130 transports. As the months went by, Pizzagalli's list of equipment expanded to include a 5,500-pound bulldozer and steel reinforcing panels that totaled 6,000 pounds to shore up the sides of the shaft.

Taylor had several concerns, which he frequently expressed to Epps and Brooks. The bulldozer, he argued, was sure to sink in the soft snow, and if reinforcing panels were necessary, wood was an acceptable substitute for steel. Taylor was also convinced that disposing of tons of excavated snow and ice would prove to be a lot harder than simply pumping meltwater from under the Gopher. He had been working closely with Bobbie Bailey on a new meltdown unit that would use a plastic pipe sunk down a probe hole as a guidance system to stop it from veering off course, and both he and Bailey were convinced the system would work.

"We've been going on camping trips before this," Epps told Taylor. "So we bored

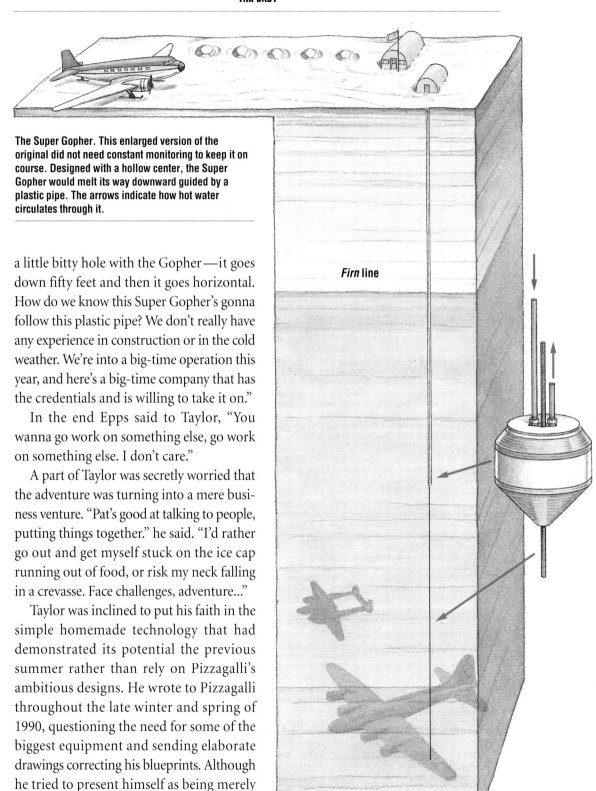

The Super Gopher. This enlarged version of the original did not need constant monitoring to keep it on course. Designed with a hollow center, the Super Gopher would melt its way downward guided by a plastic pipe. The arrows indicate how hot water circulates through it.

Firn line

a little bitty hole with the Gopher — it goes down fifty feet and then it goes horizontal. How do we know this Super Gopher's gonna follow this plastic pipe? We don't really have any experience in construction or in the cold weather. We're into a big-time operation this year, and here's a big-time company that has the credentials and is willing to take it on."

In the end Epps said to Taylor, "You wanna go work on something else, go work on something else. I don't care."

A part of Taylor was secretly worried that the adventure was turning into a mere business venture. "Pat's good at talking to people, putting things together." he said. "I'd rather go out and get myself stuck on the ice cap running out of food, or risk my neck falling in a crevasse. Face challenges, adventure..."

Taylor was inclined to put his faith in the simple homemade technology that had demonstrated its potential the previous summer rather than rely on Pizzagalli's ambitious designs. He wrote to Pizzagalli throughout the late winter and spring of 1990, questioning the need for some of the biggest equipment and sending elaborate drawings correcting his blueprints. Although he tried to present himself as being merely helpful, Taylor felt that Pizzagalli wasn't

Friends and family see off the 1990 GES expedition from Atlanta's DeKalb-Peachtree Airport.

they looked like an athletic team. Epps downed two fast glasses of wine and delivered a funny, extemporaneous speech that mimicked the rolling cadences and controlled hysteria of an evangelist. ("We're all goin' up to Koo-loo-sook. Everybody say Koo-loo-sook. No, louder! KOO-LOO-SOOK!")

The next morning Epps and Taylor negotiated the final agreement with Pizzagalli. Epps had persuaded the original investors to relinquish their claim to the second plane, which went instead to Pizzagalli (after the third was up). If fewer than three planes were recovered, then Pizzagalli got 30 per cent of any book, television or film rights. At one point Taylor started to add, "If you don't perform..." and Pizzagalli quickly corrected him. It was a diplomatic blunder that foreshadowed the gulf that would develop between GES and the Pizzagalli crew.

Bad weather dogged the GES advance party for two weeks. Since Epps had sold the Cessna rather than purchase the more efficient but costly new skis it needed, he was flying with Buzz Kaplan, the retired owner of a multimillion-dollar Minnesota-based tool company, who had agreed to ferry the advance party to the ice cap in his high-performance Cessna ski-plane. Between Sondre Stromfjord and Kulusuk, they had trouble with their navigation system and ended up flying in a huge arc. Precariously low on fuel, they radioed the nearest airport, but it was fogged in. A passing airliner, overhearing their predicament, directed them to a frozen lake where they made an emergency landing. Later a helicopter arrived with a barrel of gas and Epps and Kaplan returned to Sondre Stromfjord. It made for a good yarn later —

sensitive to GES's financial and technical limitations, and wasn't drawing upon the valuable arctic experience that he and Epps had amassed. Pizzagalli was annoyed that Taylor was telling him how to do his job. Although he'd grudgingly agreed that running a small-scale Gopher operation was acceptable, he was adamant that the focus of the expedition be concentrated on his professional excavation project.

Epps and Taylor moved further apart on this issue than they had on anything else during the long years of their friendship. Epps shared with Brooks a feeling of absolute confidence in Pizzagalli, and he believed that when you engage a man of Pizzagalli's stature and experience, you have to trust his judgment. At the same time, he thought some of what Taylor was saying made sense, and he, too, was watching nervously as Pizzagalli's project grew in scale.

On Thursday, May 3, after a round of media interviews, Epps and Taylor flew to Burlington with a few other GES members for dinner with the Pizzagalli brothers, their families and some of their crew. Dressed in GES sweatshirts, peaked caps and jackets,

Once they were back on the ice, the same old routines asserted themselves. This year, however, there was more equipment to unload than ever before and more people to help.

Epps's wife, Ann, and his daughter, Elaine, had t-shirts made up that read, "Sonde-to-Sonde the hard way"—but no one had to point out that it was the closest brush with tragedy yet.

On Sunday, May 13, the weather cleared and the advance party landed on the ice cap. As usual, all signs of the previous year's camp had been covered by snow. Using a hand-held transit and instinct, Gordon Scott chose what felt like the right spot. "You're out of your mind," Epps said. "This ain't it. You're half a mile off."

Deferring to Scott's experience, they set up camp anyway. (Two weeks later, as the surface of the ice cap dropped two feet in the warm summer temperatures, a triumphant Scott showed Epps the top of the previous year's flag pole, which popped out of the snow between their tents.) They dug holes

between four and six feet deep and pitched their domed tents in a long row, facing away from the relentless northwest Greenland wind. The Icelanders — Jon Sveinsson and Addi Hermannsson — were first, next to Epps and Taylor who were beside Scott and Neil Estes. Farther down the row, Norman Vaughan and Dr. Dan Callahan pitched their tent. Photographer Lou Sapienza's tent was next, beside a tent belonging to a two-man German film crew shooting a documentary on the expedition.

The last tent belonged to Doug Epps, Pat's older brother. Gruff, engaging, built like an aging football tackle, the gregarious Epps was having

Pat's brother Doug Epps was the GES's resident jester and its most experienced pilot.

129

A ski-equipped C-130 Hercules belonging to the New York National Guard taxis in with more equipment. (Opposite page) Angelo Pizzagalli (in camouflage) directs his group of volunteers in using the silo unloader.

his customary wonderful time, chatting up pilots and barmaids in Kulusuk and cutting up for the German filmmakers by telling war stories and corny jokes, playing his harmonica and blowing his hand-carved train whistle. It was his fourth trip to Greenland, and even though he relished his role as GES's clown prince, he was by far the most experienced pilot among them, having recently retired after thirty-two-years with Delta Airlines. Latterly a captain on L-1011 jumbo jets, the bulky Epps was affectionately nicknamed Captain Widebody.

In preparation for the arrival of the C-130s, Taylor and Scott, under the watchful eye of Lieutenant Colonel Ray Tousey, laid out a mile-long runway bordered by black markers placed at 500-foot intervals. Tousey, an experienced C-130 pilot, was to approve the runway and direct the landings. They tried to flatten the snow using snowmobiles, but Tousey told them that the C-130 pilots couldn't risk landing the large four-engine transports unless the surface was smoother.

Without the equipment being brought by the C-130s, the expedition

would have to be canceled. The only solution seemed to be taxiing the DC-3 up and down the runway to flatten it out with the plane's wide skis. It was a calculated risk. The DC-3 couldn't be taxied for too long, Bob Harless and Neil Estes warned, because it wouldn't get enough air through its oil coolers to cool the engines properly. And blowing an engine in Greenland could be catastrophic. After discussing it at length, Epps, Taylor and Brooks decided to take the risk. At 4:00 P.M. on Monday, May 21, the first C-130 lumbered onto what had been dubbed the Don Brooks International Airport. Four flights later, sixty thousand pounds of cargo lay on the ice cap.

By then Pizzagalli's crew had arrived — mainly young volunteers whom Taylor described as "full of piss and vinegar with plenty of enthusiasm." In a flurry of activity over the next few days, the Pizzagalli operation began to take shape. A huge tent with a cathedral ceiling sheltered the

(Below) The tent over the Pizzagalli operation.

Pizzagalli's undertaking was incredibly ambitious. After the silo unloader blades (left) had broken up the snow, it was loaded into a sack (below left) and dumped outside the hole. A small bulldozer was used to get rid of the snow once it was dug out, and plywood sheeting was needed to keep the sides of the shaft from falling in (below right).

silo unloader which, thanks to two diesel generators driving powerful electric motors, began carving its way down to the P-38. Shredded ice was pushed to the center of the shaft, where it was blown into a large nylon bucket suspended from a heavy winch and hauled to the surface. Using the bulldozer, they piled the excavated snow and ice onto a mound that quickly became a small mountain.

One hundred yards away, the Super Gopher was melting a four-foot-diameter hole down through the ice cap over *Big Stoop*. It resembled an obese plumb bob around which copper tubing had been wound. Boiling water was pumped through the tubing and back to the surface via an outtake hose. The Super Gopher made steady progress, but at eighty feet the shaft began to flood. It had reached the *firn* line, the point at which compacted snow turns into glacier ice, losing moisture in the process. Estes borrowed a deep well pump from the Pizzagalli crew. Two days later, although the Gopher crew pumped more than four thousand gallons out of the shaft, the Super Gopher, still melting its way down, remained underwater.

Work was delayed in the early weeks by three blizzards that paralyzed Gopherville, as they had dubbed their camp. In a storm, all energy was devoted to survival. Tents had to be cleared of snow before they collapsed, which sometimes meant waking every couple of hours. At 3:30 one morning, Taylor awoke. The tent was dark and very quiet — too quiet. The nylon walls were bulging under the weight of accumulated snow, and Taylor was afraid to move for

Pat Epps and Richard Taylor wrestle the Super Gopher into place.

fear they would cave in. Beside him he felt the knife he kept just in case his tent ever did collapse and he had to cut his way out. Then he eased gingerly out of his sleeping bag and squirmed into his clothes. Unzipping the tent, he faced a solid wall of snow. Some mornings it took an hour just to dig an exit tunnel. Then more digging to sink tents deeper into protective holes. Then more digging to shore up the ice walls that served as windbreaks. Greenland's Inuit name is *Kalaallit Nunaat*. Taylor insisted the literal translation was "Shovel or Die."

When the weather cleared, the entire

Richard Taylor starts the descent to Big Stoop, as Gordon Scott, Norman Vaughan and Neil Estes stand by.

raised to the surface, repaired and lowered again so he could reattach it. Having paid his dues, he continued down the shaft.

Taylor fought back pangs of anxiety. The light on his hard hat cast an eerie beam onto the ice walls, and he had to watch vigilantly to prevent himself from becoming tangled in hoses and chains. Cold water rained down constantly, and every sound echoed liquidly.

Finally he saw the Super Gopher, covered in oil and resting in a pool of water. Using a two-way radio, he told Estes to stop. It was difficult to look down while suspended in the harness, so Taylor squirmed and shifted, dropping one of his two walkie-talkies in the process, until he was able to shine his lamp below the Gopher.

He saw a flash of yellow. It was the painted tip of a bent black propeller. The Super Gopher was resting on an engine cowling at the point where it joined the wing. There was no telling the condition of the whole plane, but when Taylor put his boot on the cowling, all he could think of were Neil Armstrong's words: *That's one small step for man, one giant leap for mankind.* Not that he had delusions about the significance of the expedition; it was just that Taylor talked a lot about pursuing impossible dreams, and none had seemed more impossible than the Lost Squadron. For Taylor, stepping onto *Big Stoop* validated his obsession.

"Richard," Doug Epps asked, after Taylor was back on the surface. "What did you find in the hole?"

Taylor turned. "One B-17E. In fair condition."

"I see a B-17."

Back on the surface, a jubilant Scott, who recorded every detail of the Super Gopher's progress in his yellow all-weather notebooks, scribbled, "1209: CONTACT - B17 'Big Stoop.'"

Later in the day, an excited Taylor strapped on a harness and Estes and Vaughan used a hand winch to lower him down the shaft. He stopped at forty feet, uncoupled the upper end of a leaking hose, and at eighty feet uncoupled the other end. Then he dangled, impatient to reach the bottom, the straps cutting uncomfortably into his groin and hips, while the hose was

(Above)
Big Stoop
reappears. The
bent propeller
here is the same
one visible
(right) in 1942.

"Fantastic," Epps said. "Any sign of damage?"

"No," Taylor said. "Prop was bent, but that happened a long time ago. Everything else looked great."

Rather than pump out the bottom of the shaft, the Super Gopher was left to warm the surrounding water in order to melt a cavity around *Big Stoop*. In the meantime, other problems emerged to temper the elation.

When the DC-3 had first arrived in Kulusuk, its number one engine had needed a new cylinder and head assembly. Now it had come in earlier in the day with the same engine smoking. Estes and Robert "Wee Gee" Smith, a member of the Pizzagalli crew and an expert mechanic, struggled to repair a master rod cylinder with limited tools in freezing temperatures. The next day, Taylor, Estes and Sapienza boarded it to fly to Kulusuk, where Taylor and Sapienza were catching connecting flights back to the U.S. With Doug Epps at the controls, the plane was hurtling along the snow when Taylor shouted, "Shut it down! Shut it down! We're on fire!" and Estes yelled, "There's smoke in the cockpit!"

Epps cut the power and coasted to a stop. Pieces of the engine were scattered along the runway. Estes and Smith worked on it for the rest of the day, repairing things sufficiently for the plane to limp back to Kulusuk, where it sat for several weeks until Pat Epps and Don Brooks arranged to have a mechanic and replacement engine flown north.

Estes, who had a moody streak, was in a stew. First Pat and Richard had okayed taxiing the DC-3 to flatten the runway,

"Wee Gee" Smith and Neil Estes working on one of the DC-3's engines.

which had surely caused the engine burnout. Then, while they were making repairs, Pizzagalli refused to lend them some welding equipment to free up a cracked spark plug. They'd dug it out, but doing it that way always leaves behind some metal filings, which may have caused the engine to go when it did. In his journal Estes wrote, "The result…is that we have finally managed to render the most useful and effective tool we have totally useless…I'm not even angry anymore — mostly it's disgust. The extreme abuse that the DC-3 has absorbed since leaving [DeKalb-Peachtree] on May 3 has finally resulted in a ruined engine and no transportation of personnel or fuel off and on the ice cap."

The Pizzagalli crew was out of sorts as well. They'd managed to carve a forty-foot hole, but both their silo unloader and their electric winches kept breaking down. Taylor was worried about safety. With Pizzagalli tending to business back in Vermont, he'd seen some of the young crew working around the hole without hard hats or safety harnesses. At dinner one evening, when the mood seemed relatively congenial, Taylor appealed to everyone to observe safety practices. Later, as he and Scott walked to their tents, Taylor asked him how he'd thought his speech had been received.

"It was okay," Scott replied. "Those guys

probably bought it, but it wasn't you."

When Taylor asked him what he meant, Scott said, "You talk all that shit to those guys but it's not your M.O. You'd go straight back to our hole and start putting people down it without changing a thing."

A chastened Taylor crawled inside his tent. He had been tormenting himself for much of the expedition about leadership and motivation. He often felt angered at what he perceived as Scott and Estes's casual attitude toward work in the Gopher tent, a sense that his friends weren't throwing themselves into the fray with the same urgency that he was. Yet when he analyzed what was being done, he saw only remarkable achievements executed cooperatively. He chastised himself for his shortcomings as a leader and a friend.

He knew Scott was right. In the excitement of the moment, he was as likely to be careless as anyone. When it came down to it, succeeding took precedence over everything else. On the way to Greenland, Estes had accused Taylor of overloading the DC-3 beyond maximum gross and flying without a heater or defroster in weather so foul they should have been grounded. Sure, we're on a budget, Estes had said, but we're pushing our luck and one time it's going to run out. Taylor was sympathetic, but as one of the co-leaders he felt he understood the overall picture. Trying to get the overloaded DC-3 off the ground was easy compared with keeping the Greenland Expedition Society aloft. They sometimes flew the DC-3 low on gas, but GES was running on fumes.

Who was right, Taylor wondered, he or Estes? As he wrote in his journal, "If nothing goes wrong, I am. If somebody gets hurt or worse, he is. I only know we gotta keep as close to the edge as possible. The margins are slim."

IT WAS IRONIC THAT ON THE GREENLAND ICE cap, in one of the coldest regions of the world, the expedition would be crippled because the weather was too warm.

In mid-July, with temperatures rising to record highs, the summer sun began melting the surface snow, creating a water table at the eighty-foot *firn* level. Glacial runoff poured into the Gopher shaft at a rate of 5,500 gallons per hour — 1,500 more than their three pumps running simultaneously could handle. The Pizzagalli shaft, now 120 feet deep, also began flooding, even with three pumps running. When the water shut down the electric silo unloader, the crew tried using chain saws to cut the ice into sections that were sledgehammered loose and lifted chunk by chunk into the bucket. Operating chain saws while standing in a foot of water on ice was declared too dangerous to continue. Soon a roaring Niagara of glacial melt pouring down from the *firn* line left twenty feet of frigid water in the hole. At the same time the bulldozer, which had been used to move the enormous loads of excavated ice, could only be used at night because its tracks bogged down in the slushy daytime snow.

The tensions that had been simmering for weeks suddenly intensified when the crews became idle. One hotheaded Pizzagalli crew member threatened to attack Gordon Scott over some minor dispute. On July 29

Gordon Scott prepares to descend to Big Stoop.

Estes wrote in his journal, "Animosity and misunderstanding between camps has grown to point that everyone is walking on eggs trying to keep from offending each other." Finally Epps, Taylor and Pizzagalli elected to send everyone off the ice cap for a vacation, leaving a skeleton crew behind.

By the second week of August, temperatures began to fall. With the pumps on, the water level in the Gopher shaft dropped. By August 15 the crews were back on the ice cap and back to work.

A week later Scott and Estes descended to *Big Stoop* together. They had identified the engine as the number two, which meant they were on the left wing not far from the cockpit. Using hot-water hoses, they began melting through the ice in the direction of the fuselage. Suddenly Estes, who was chipping at some ice, called to Scott, "God, you're not gonna believe this." The barrel of a .50-caliber machine gun in the ball turret poked ominously from the

ice. At that discovery, Estes and Scott whooped and howled like schoolboys. In lieu of Champagne and caviar, they celebrated with what they had: water and fig newtons.

Two days later Scott took the eighty-five-year-old Norman Vaughan down the shaft to visit the bomber that he'd last seen nearly half a century earlier. Four hours later Estes helped Vaughan out of the shaft. Vaughan, a veteran of five Greenland expeditions who had devoted much of his life to adventures of one kind or another turned to Estes and said, "That was one of the greatest experiences of my life."

On August 31, after nine years of dreaming about the Lost Squadron, Pat Epps was lowered down the shaft, followed by Scott and Taylor. As they neared the bottom, voices echoed spookily and naked bulbs cast a garish light that reflected crazily off the ice and the pools of water that collected between fragments of metal. The steady

Using pressurized steam and hot water, they melted away a cavern around the bomber.

Pat Epps examines Big Stoop. Half a century in a glacier had literally ground the plane apart.

drone of the deep well pump was reassuring, Taylor thought. That's the only thing keeping the melting glacier from refilling this frozen grotto like a freshly flushed toilet bowl.

Epps and Scott, clad in bright orange slickers and hard hats, touched down first. Their movements were tentative as they picked their way around the ice and metal. Dangling ten feet above them, Taylor was struck by the surreal sight: they looked like subterranean spies in a James Bond thriller.

A few minutes later Taylor stood on the number two engine cowling. The air was musty and damp, a stale mixture of carbon dioxide and engine oil. Scott and Estes had melted a triangular cavern about twenty feet long sloping to a fifteen-foot apex. The bomber could be seen floating in a pool of glacial melt, from about three feet in front of the cockpit windscreen to ten feet behind the ball turret.

After the first flush of excitement, Taylor's heart sank, even though he'd been warned by Scott and Estes what to expect. Although a few individual parts were relatively intact, most of *Big Stoop* was a jumble of crushed and mangled junk. Under his feet, he could see that the number two engine had moved several inches forward, severing the engine mounts, linkages, wires and fuel lines. The roof of the cockpit was squashed to below the level of the pilot's and copilot's seats, their controls protruding through the aluminum skin. Only the top ball turret remained intact, its pair

Dressed in an aviator's helmet and white scarf, Gordon Scott hams it up for the camera atop Big Stoop. The turret in front of him was about the only part of the plane still readily recognizable (inset).

of .50-caliber machine guns pointing aft. Everything was approximately where it should have been, but airplanes are not approximate pieces of technology. As Neil had described it, it was as though a giant had put all the plane's parts in a bag, shaken it violently, then arranged the parts in roughly their original position.

Slowly the three men began cataloging the plane, videotaping it and snapping photographs. They were thrilled to find the names "Marion" and "Dorothy" perfectly preserved in black lettering on either side of the ball turret. Later Epps sat where the pilot's seat should have been, with Taylor beside him as copilot and Scott at the bombardier's post. They took turns posing for pictures in an aviator's leather helmet and white scarf. Then they began removing pieces of the aircraft to be winched to the surface.

Scott led daily scavenging trips to *Big Stoop*, removing an assortment of salvageable gear, including the throttle quadrant, the control yokes, the emergency bomb

(Right) Richard Taylor beside Big Stoop. The machine gun (above) and control yoke (inset) were among the items salvaged from the bomber.

release, miscellaneous radio and navigation instruments, identification plates, oxygen masks, flying boots, Lucky Strike tobacco tins, the pilot's and copilot's seats, the .50-caliber machine guns and hundreds of rounds of ammunition. Since the plane was unsalvageable and therefore of no interest to the GES investors, and Brooks had spent more than $600,000 financing most of the '89 expedition and his share of '90, the B-17 was declared his. Brooks was happy to take the historical booty, but he thought of it as serving the best interests of GES rather than as buying an aircraft, considering B-17s in flying condition sold for $500,000 or less.

Despite protests from Scott and Estes, at the end of the summer, Epps, Taylor and Brooks agreed to Pizzagalli's request that the Super Gopher be moved to the P-38 hole. It melted a fifty-foot shaft — putting it less than a hundred feet from the aircraft — before breaking down. With very little time remaining before the winter storms began, Pizzagalli officially canceled the operation. A caretaker crew was left behind to help the GES team evacuate the camp.

That proved more difficult than anyone had imagined. Early in August Iraq invaded Kuwait. The American military buildup for what would ultimately be known as Desert Storm began, and the C-130s scheduled to retrieve their equipment — especially Pizzagalli's enormous generators and bulldozer — were indefinitely diverted to the Persian Gulf.

Fate was working against them close by as well. A few weeks earlier, as Epps was beginning his takeoff in the DC-3, Estes, who was standing with Scott beside the runway, heard the number two engine rattling like stones on a tin roof. "That engine's history," he said, watching carefully as the plane gained speed. Just as it lifted off, the engine burst into flames, forming an orange fireball. Grabbing the two-way radio from Scott, Estes called, "Pat, you're on fire!"

"How bad?" Epps asked, unable to see the engine from the pilot's seat.

"You're a mile away and I can see it as clear as day."

Epps waited another fifteen seconds, then shut down the engine. Leaving a trail of black smoke, he managed to fly on one overheated engine one hundred miles to Kulusuk, where he made an emergency landing. No one knew how long it was going to take to get another DC-3 engine flown to Greenland.

By mid-September the site was abandoned, most of the heavy equipment stored in tents to be picked up at an unspecified future time. A few weeks later Don Brooks and Bob Harless flew from Douglas to Kulusuk with a DC-3 engine, spoiling a bet among the locals at the airport over who would get rich storing the aircraft for the winter. After mounting the new engine, the locals laid bets with each other that Brooks and Harless wouldn't make it back to Atlanta. When they did, Brooks heard that the winner made enough money to start his own satellite television business.

YEARS LATER EPPS AND TAYLOR STOOD IN the conference room of Epps Aviation, showing a visitor a framed photo hanging on the wall. It was Epps standing on the runway at Kulusuk in August 1990. Behind him was a DC-3 engine that looked like it had been struck by antiaircraft fire. On his face he wore the maniacal smile of a man who has cheated death.

"They call that my 'shit-eatin' ' grin," said Epps, chuckling.

"Luck's played a significant part in everything we did," Taylor said. "We were vulnerable in any number of ways. We would sometimes carry one, two or three thousand pounds more load than the DC-3 was certified to carry, which means if you lose an engine you're gonna crash. We were lucky nobody got seriously hurt going down that shaft, working around that plane."

Taylor flashed his best daredevil grin. "There's an old saying that pretty much sums up our expeditions: 'Smart's good, luck's better.'"

Holding the flag of the Explorers Club, Taylor and Epps pose for the camera.

CHAPTER FIVE

DREAMERS OF THE DAY

AT EPPS AND RICHARD TAYLOR SMILED self-consciously into the camera as they held the piece of *Big Stoop* bearing the words "Phyllis Arleen." The name had been painted in 1942 by the plane's pilot, Joe Hanna, in honor of his wife. Millions of Americans tuned in to NBC's "Today" show on Wednesday, November 28, 1990, to watch as Epps and Taylor handed the battered memento over to Hanna's elderly widow, an elegant woman wearing a simple black dress and a string of pearls. She in turn presented Epps and Taylor with the keys to the door of the bomber, which she had kept in her basement for decades.

Pat Epps, Don Brooks and Richard Taylor present Phyllis Hanna with the piece of Big Stoop that had her name on it. (Opposite) After the 1990 expedition, it seemed unlikely that the GES would ever make camp again on the ice cap.

"Mr. Epps, Mr. Taylor," said Deborah Norville, co-host of "Today" at the time. "I know the adventure is only just beginning but we look forward to seeing the final chapter in a few more years."

What Norville didn't know was that the adventurers were despondent and, far from beginning, the adventure seemed to be over. It had been nearly a decade since they'd first ventured to Greenland and now, three months after returning from the 1990 expedition, they were awash in debt. GES owed a total of $750,000 to investors, lawyers, the air force and other creditors, and the Pizzagalli brothers were holding the society responsible for getting their equipment off the ice cap or reimbursing them for its loss. As for the expedition itself, even Epps and Taylor had lost their optimism. GES had found a wrecked, unsalvageable B-17 while Pizzagalli's construction firm, which had extensive cold-weather experience, had only made it three-quarters of the way to the real treasure, a P-38. How could they convince potential investors that the P-38s were salvageable and likely to be in better shape than the bomber? They didn't fully believe it themselves. As a dejected Taylor confided to his wife, "Nancy, it looks like it's over."

Or not. Soon Epps, Taylor and Don

Brooks were back at the Downwind, buoying each other's hopes. They had proven that they could reach a plane using the Gopher technology. Furthermore, there was an encouraging groundswell of support from across the country and abroad. Over the previous few years, GES had received hundreds of letters from aviation enthusiasts, history buffs and people eager to support the twin causes of adventure and exploration. So many letters contained unsolicited contributions that they'd established "The Lightning Brigade," which had four hundred members by the end of 1990. For contributions ranging from $25 to $25,000, donors received an honorary rank and were entitled to one of many mementos ranging from patches, caps and videos to watches, leather flight jackets and trips to the ice cap. Sensing a profit-making venture, they'd hired a marketing director named Bob Pope, who made his living merchandising collegiate sportswear, to try to interest J. C. Penney and other national and regional retailers to carry GES merchandise. However low they felt, the story hadn't lost its ability to captivate, to excite others as it had once excited them.

Most of all there was the nagging question. As Brooks put it one day after ordering another round of drinks, "Whut if we don't go back and somebody else goes down to a P-38 in a year or two and it's salvageable and they bring it back and make it fly? How we gonna feel 'bout that?"

"You're right," Taylor said. "There are eight airplanes up there and we hit the bad one."

"Yeah," agreed Epps. "The P-38s are smaller and tougher. They're probably perfect."

But despite the many friends donating their time and talents, and the many small donations, they needed a big sponsor. Over the next few months, everyone went to work trying to generate interest in the project. Lockheed and Boeing were approached again, as was R. J. Reynolds. Epps contacted the celebrated aviation writer Ernest K. Gann, author of such best-selling books as *The High and the Mighty* and *Fate Is the Hunter*. He figured that if someone of Gann's stature wrote the story of the Lost Squadron, GES would earn a percentage of the sales as well as a piece of any film deal. "I would be very interested..." Gann wrote, "but until some kind of 'story-end' is realized there is not much I can do about it." Gann suggested contacting Thomas Watson, Jr., an aviation buff who had built his father's firm, IBM, into a corporate giant. Epps sent Watson a brochure, a video and a letter.

A few weeks later Watson wrote back: "I think it's an unusual endeavor which will give all of you lots of adventure and satisfaction. On the other hand...it isn't anything that would interest me."

Then Epps contacted Nashville-based Textron Aerostructures, a major aerospace firm that made components for Titan IV missiles and assorted structures for military and commercial aircraft. What excited Epps, however, was the fact that Textron had built P-38s for Lockheed during the war. Textron's marketing executives were enthusiastic about the project and, in order to guarantee that a sponsor would own the first plane, Epps and Taylor renegotiated their salvage rights with the Danish government so that instead of the first plane, the Danes would receive a "significant display" of photographs and artifacts for their museum.

No one was sure what happened next, but as Epps understood it, "a boss man at Textron" was surprised to hear about the company's involvement in the scheme and canceled it. Despite considerable interest in the project — the German documentary on the Lost Squadron had aired in Germany and was being marketed in other countries; Epps and Taylor were talking to *National Geographic* and *Explorer* about articles; Ernest Gann was still a possible author for a book — GES found itself sponsorless again. By Christmas, with the May departure date for the 1992 trip only four months away, the expedition was no more ready to fly than the P-38s buried in the ice cap.

As it happened, the answer to their problems had shown up in the offices of Epps Aviation in September 1990, just after Epps had returned from the ice cap. His name was Roy Shoffner. When he had come to call, the usually ebullient Epps had been visibly depressed. Not only had the expedition been a failure, but his brother Doug had died in his sleep a few weeks earlier. Epps had set Shoffner up in front of a TV set to watch a couple of GES videos and told him to look at the artifacts from the B-17 on display in the lobby. Shoffner, who had learned about the Lost Squadron through aviation magazines, was struck by the fact that Epps didn't try to solicit money or even ask him how he wanted to get involved.

"Pat," Shoffner said, "after spending all this money and all this time, what have you got?"

"Just a bag of memories," Epps replied matter of factly.

Shoffner didn't think too much more about GES after that, but the story still intrigued him. One thing Shoffner loved was flying. He owned several small planes that he kept in hangars at tiny Middlesboro Airport, and he enjoyed the company of fellow fliers. Wherever he went he would ask people what ideas they had for getting the aircraft out of the glacier.

For Shoffner, these were more than idle thoughts. A millionaire who lived near Middlesboro, Kentucky, a small town that was a mere hour from Atlanta as the Cessna flies, Shoffner had strong entrepreneurial instincts. In college he earned money by taking pictures of couples at weekend dances with his Crown Graphic, developing them in his home darkroom over the weekend and selling them at school on Monday. After a stint in the air

Roy Shoffner shown with his wife, Eddie Lou.

force piloting F-89 interceptors, he returned to Middlesboro and began working for a plastics manufacturer.

In 1971 he started Duraline Corporation, a company that manufactured plastic water pipe, and as a sideline over the years he built and operated fast-food restaurants, supermarkets and commercial properties. When the telephone industry switched to fiber-optic cable, Duraline produced a specially designed plastic conduit that cornered the market. In 1985, when he was fifty-seven years old, Shoffner was approached by a New York firm that liked his business better than he did. He sold Duraline for $10 million, remaining on a retainer for five years. By 1991 he was keeping himself busy in civic affairs and dabbling in a few business ventures, but was pretty much free to do with his life as he pleased.

A couple of months after Shoffner visited Epps, Don Brooks and Bob Pope were talking up GES at the annual Sun 'n' Fun air show in Florida when someone mentioned a rich fellow in Kentucky who seemed keen on the project. Pope contacted Shoffner, who said he was still interested.

Over the next nine months, Epps and Brooks talked with Shoffner many times, in person and over the phone. Finally, on February 4, 1992, they reached an agreement, outlined in a three-page contract drawn up without the annoying meddling of attorneys. Shoffner, operating as Pinnacle Airways, agreed to lend GES $350,000, interest free, to mount an expedition. The goal was three P-38s, with the intention of restoring the best two to flying condition.

(Privately, Epps suspected they'd be lucky to recover one.) The cost of returning the aircraft to the U.S. was to be divided equally, as were the proceeds from selling the plane after Shoffner's $350,000 had been repaid. As for restoring the planes, the agreement read, "A plan must be agreed to by both parties that it is financially beneficial to rebuild the plane(s). If an agreement cannot be reached, one party may make an offer for the plane(s) and the other party will either buy or sell at that price."

As a legal document the contract was little more than a handshake in writing, but neither GES nor Shoffner wanted to get into contractual wrangling, and everyone involved felt that a simple contract was in keeping with the spirit of cooperation and adventure that they liked to feel had been the founding principle of the search eleven years earlier.

Around this time, Epps received a call from Bob Cardin, who had spent some time on the ice cap in 1990 as investor Pete Mallen's corporate pilot. Epps had been impressed by Cardin's take-charge manner and had asked him whether he'd like to manage GES's next expedition. Cardin had agreed, but then the '91 expedition hadn't materialized. Cardin had left Mallen's company and was now wondering whether Epps knew of any openings for a pilot. Instead, Epps told him GES had just found financing and the 1992 expedition was going to leave in early May. Would he like to come on board?

To call Cardin a corporate pilot, in the sense that many corporate pilots are little

more than jet-age chauffeurs, would be misleading. A forty-six-year-old native of Rhode Island, he had degrees in education and military science. He joined the army in 1968, flew Hueys in Vietnam, and after returning to the U.S., worked his way up through the military ranks, serving as an operations officer, an instructor-pilot and an adviser to the New Hampshire Air National Guard. In the early 1980s he ran a U.S. installation in Puerto Rico and later became airfield commander at Fort Devens in Massachusetts, retiring a lieutenant colonel in 1988. Then he went to work for

Mallen Industries, a textile company, as a pilot. Pete Mallen, who became a close friend, promoted him to plant manager, which suited Cardin's skills but not his inclinations.

Epps named Cardin "project coordinator," a catchall title Gordon Scott had held in previous years. For a salary of $3,500 a month up to departure and $4,000 a month on the ice cap, Cardin would be responsible for organizing and running the expedition.

One thing made Cardin uncomfortable. Although he was in charge of the camp, Gordon Scott was to run the Gopher operation. It was almost as if they were co-leaders. Then, at a GES shareholders' meeting on Friday, February 21, Cardin got what he thought was an explanation of his position. After he had outlined his military career, Bobbie Bailey asked him who would be in charge on the ice cap.

"When I was an airfield commander," he explained, "I ran the airfield for the general, not for myself. If a private needs to know something about running the airfield, he doesn't ask the general, he asks me.

"I equate that to the ice cap. I'm taking care of day-to-day decision-making and getting the airplane up for Pat and Richard, the founders of GES. If there's something they don't like, they come to me to get it done rather than go solve the problem themselves."

Bailey appeared to be satisfied with that answer, Cardin thought, and Epps, who was also present, leaned back in his chair and flashed him thumbs up. To Cardin it seemed that, in the event of a standoff on

Bob Cardin was hired to serve as project coordinator for the 1992 expedition.

the ice cap, final authority was his.

From that moment on, Cardin had his work cut out for him. He and Don Brooks had eight weeks to draft a plan and either purchase or design and manufacture all necessary equipment, then test it, package it and ship it. Using a spare warehouse in Douglas belonging to Brooks, Cardin and Brooks assembled storage and crew tents, a new Gopher tent and mess hall, hundreds of feet of plastic and steel pipes, boilers, generators, the steam probe with its high-pressure hose and tips of various sizes, countless bits and pieces of hardware and tools and all of the food supplies. (Bobbie Bailey's Our-Way was responsible for supplying the new, improved Super Gopher III, which Cardin was to pick up en route to Greenland.) Cardin also consulted by phone with Gordon Scott and Neil Estes.

Given that they planned to dismantle a P-38 under the ice and bring it up piece by piece, Cardin was surprised that no one had precise data on the size and weight of all its parts. How could he figure out the number of Gopher holes needed, the strength of the frame, the lifting power of the winches? But with just sixty days to put the expedition together, he decided that it made more sense to rely on the know-how that GES had collected over the years rather than question everything. So he and Brooks made educated guesses and beefed up most of the equipment just to be safe.

At the beginning of May, Cardin and all his cargo arrived in an air force transport plane at Sondre Stromfjord, where he arranged with local military officials for it to be shuttled to Kulusuk. The largest and most ambitious GES expedition to date was under way.

EPPS AND TAYLOR ARRIVED IN SONDE ON Wednesday, May 6, along with a dozen members of the expedition. After dinner they went for a walk to discuss the first glitch in their plans. Gordon Scott should have been on the ice cap already with Bil Thuma to pinpoint the planes with Thuma's radar, but they were stranded by bad weather in Iceland. Reasoning that early in the expedition it was better to take a step forward — even a risky one — than make no progress at all, Epps and Taylor decided that Taylor should take five men to the site and create a beachhead in the approximate area of the camp.

The next morning Taylor overheard a passionate discussion outside the door of his room. Neil Estes was telling Don Brooks that it was crazy and possibly dangerous to drop six people on the ice cap to set up a camp that would have to be moved later when the planes were located by radar. What if a blizzard hit and they were marooned there for a week? They had too few provisions and no backup plans. Brooks seemed in agreement, and Taylor could hear other members of the expedition chipping in, getting increasingly agitated. Finally Taylor gathered everyone together and heard them out. An hour later Epps showed up. "We're gonna drop six guys off," he said. "The rest of you'll come to Kulusuk. Let's go."

"Wait a minute, Pat," Taylor said. "We're having a discussion here and there are some views I think you ought to hear."

Taylor presented all sides of the argument clearly, emphasizing everyone's concern for safety. When he was finished, Epps nodded. "That's good. I'm glad you guys figured it all out. Now pack up your stuff and let's get going."

"Does that mean we're going to Kulusuk?" someone piped up.

"Yup," Epps replied on his way out the door. "Right after we drop the guys on the ice cap."

There were a few grumbles, but everyone packed his gear and headed for the DC-3. That was the essence of their partnership, Taylor thought. He was the "participant-explainer" — someone who listened to everyone's views and tried to achieve a consensus within the group. Epps, on the other hand, was a "delegator-disappearer." He used the force of his personality and his infectious energy to get people on board, then made his decision and was gone before anyone had time to question him.

It was mid-afternoon, a clear, bright day, by the time the DC-3 left Sonde. Three hours later, having located the approximate area using satellite navigational aids, Epps circled while everyone tried in vain to see evidence of the 1990 camp. After dropping off the advance team, the DC-3 lumbered into the sky. Since Scott and Thuma had made it into Kulusuk that afternoon, Epps said he'd return with them a couple of hours later, but he was no sooner out of sight than the drone of the engines returned. Circling overhead, Epps radioed to Taylor that the Kulusuk airport wouldn't remain open

long enough for him to make another trip that day. Finally Epps mentioned that he'd accidentally dropped them on top of a snow-bridge covering a crevasse, so they'd better move a couple of hundred yards.

The wind was picking up and the temperature was dropping fast, so Taylor instructed everyone to dig in and pitch the tents. That night the wind gusted to fifty miles per hour. Taylor lay awake listening to the tent flap rattling and the nylon fabric heaving up and down like a sprinter's lung.

S HORTLY AFTER NOON THE NEXT DAY, THE DC-3 landed at the site. With Scott and Thuma was David Kaufman, a thirty-three-year-old mechanical engineer from Atlanta on his first trip to the ice cap. Landing in Kulusuk had put Kaufman in culture shock; stepping down onto the glacier stunned him. The wind blew snow across the barren surface of the ice cap and the cold penetrated every opening in his winter clothing. Taylor met the plane, but the rest of the advance party remained in their tents for several minutes before finally emerging to help unload. Although they had only spent one night, Kaufman observed, they already looked worn out. What had he gotten

David Kaufman was stunned at the severity of the Greenland storms.

himself into? He felt as though he had been dropped on the forbidding frozen planet where Captain Kirk battled Ricardo Montalban in the second *Star Trek* movie, *The Wrath of Khan.*

While Kaufman and the others dug in, Scott and Thuma, noting that the tents seemed to be at least half a mile from the 1990 site, dropped their gear and hiked into the distance with the survey instruments. With so much heavy equipment and people due, they knew it was vital to relocate the

A single night's snowfall outside the mess tent door.

camp. But he and Thuma were so absorbed in their surveying calculations that they failed to notice the telltale signs of an approaching storm: the distant peaks from which they had just taken angular measurements had disappeared from sight. By the time they found their way back to the camp, the wind was whistling across the ice cap at nearly seventy-five miles per hour and the gusting snow made it impossible to see farther than ten feet.

Scott and Thuma spent the next three hours feverishly shoveling a hole and wind wall so they could pitch their tent. Why, Thuma wondered, had he left pleasant spring weather in Toronto for this? He and Scott were exhausted and soaked with sweat, their balaclavas frozen solid to their beards. Ice covered Thuma's glasses so thickly he couldn't see. As he dug, he asked himself why an advance party had been dropped before the radar arrived. And why did the shovels have long, highly varnished handles that slipped and turned over when gripped by frozen mittens? *Good ol' Georgia shovels*, Thuma fumed. *Probably used for planting cotton and bought in a goddamn hardware store in Atlanta!*

In a calmer moment, he wrote in his journal, "GES observations — well, still not tight organization but better much better than '88. It's sometimes like a 'happening' waiting for fate to make decisions..."

The next morning a badly rattled Kaufman crawled out of his tent, his clothing still caked with snow and ice. The neighboring tents were nearly buried, so he helped his colleagues dig their way out. He noticed that Scott and Thuma's tent was perfectly sunk into its hole, where a wind wall had protected it from the worst of the snow. Late the previous night, when the wind was hitting Kaufman's hood so hard his goggles rattled on his face, he had admitted to Scott that he was coming unglued. "It's just wind," Scott calmly told him. As another storm rolled across the ice cap, Kaufman realized that to survive, you watched Gordon Scott and did whatever he did. Scott seemed to be the expedition's true leader.

The following Monday, May 11, Taylor boarded the DC-3 for Kulusuk and from there returned to Atlanta, where his over-extended architectural partnership was beginning to slide into trouble. Having endured ferocious winds and tons of accumulated snow all week, the expeditioners looked shell-shocked but, as Taylor was delighted to observe, they were gamely persevering against the odds. In his journal he wrote, "In 5 days we've located the planes, moved camp ½ mile, erected 6 structures and 5 tents, unloaded, moved and stored 12 tons of equipment, weathered a severe storm and drunk a whole bottle of scotch. What a team!"

A ROUND THE TIME TAYLOR LEFT, BOB Cardin and Roy Shoffner arrived on the ice cap. Cardin's first impression was that the camp was running in slow motion. His first task was to get things whipped into shape. No detail could be overlooked.

"What's the mess schedule?" he asked a surprised Lou Sapienza.

Sapienza, the photographer who had

been along on the previous two expeditions, was the official cook. As he understood it, the Greenland Expedition Society was a pretty casual operation, an extension of the old "summer camp for the boys" spirit of years ago. Besides, most of the expeditioners were still a bit wrung out from the intensity of the first week's storm. Work was getting done, but nobody punched a clock. Sapienza told Cardin that meals took place at about the same time every day — breakfast was at around ten, dinner at eight and lunch was whenever it happened.

Roy Shoffner arrived at the site in mid-May.

"Breakfast is going to be at 0700 to 0800," Cardin said sharply, his shoulders braced. "Lunch will be 1200 to 1300. Dinner 1700 to 1800."

"I'd like you to put that in writing," Sapienza muttered.

That was Cardin's style during his first couple of weeks in the camp. He was a short, wiry man with an intense, barely contained energy that suggested a coiled spring. In his obsession with results he could be abrupt, his manner excessively authoritarian, as though he was running a boot camp rather than leading a team of civilians. But Epps had said he wanted at least one P-38 out of the ice cap by the fiftieth anniversary in mid-July, and Cardin couldn't see that happening unless someone was pushing. When his initial attempt at

The Super Gopher III starting up. (Left to right) The hoses that circulate hot water through the Gopher are hooked up and then the lowering begins. The heat of the Gopher causes steam to rise up the shaft.

Pizzagalli's bulldozer from the 1990 expedition is unearthed to be put to use in 1992.

implementing rigid schedules didn't take, though, he backed off. He reasserted himself from time to time, but there were other occasions, such as the day the steam probe hit the P-38 and Cardin brought out a bottle of Kentucky whiskey to celebrate, when his relationship with most of the crew was collegial. In his journal, Neil Estes was thinking of Cardin when he wrote, "Spirit of past expeditions isn't quite there...no real problems yet but conditions here can create clashes in personalities..."

But cozy memories of past expeditions were giving way to harsh realities. For such an ambitious, well-funded undertaking, preparations had been badly rushed. As the Gopher shelter was erected and the larger Super Gopher III was suspended from its frame, serious deficiencies in planning became apparent. Instead of good electric drills there were cheap battery-powered models. Instead of a professional carpenter's circular saw there was a home-hobbyist's version equipped with badly made, inexpensive blades. There were few extension cords, insufficient rope and many overlooked or misplaced pieces of hardware. When it was necessary to break a packing crate apart one day, Estes had to use a length of heavy pipe because there was neither a crowbar nor a sledgehammer. A pair of snowblowers proved nearly useless in ice-cap conditions, and when the snowmobile broke an axle there was no spare to repair it.

Before the end of the month, trips were made to Sondre Stromfjord and Dye 2 (another one of the DEW-line radar stations recently abandoned by the U.S. military) to scrounge materials. At Scott and Shoffner's suggestion, Wee Gee Smith, the former Pizzagalli crew member who had been invited to join the GES expedition, began digging through twenty-five feet of snow to Pizzagalli's 1990 camp to recover the bulldozer, generators, winches and other needed gear.

Dave Kaufman, who often felt that any

advice he gave was ignored, even when it concerned his specialty, complained that these kinds of details were usually dealt with during the preliminary "engineering phase" of a project. That got a good laugh, and someone repeated the line about GES's operating philosophy being "Ready, fire, aim."

Tensions soon developed between Cardin and Scott over the pace of work. Scott's wife, who was pregnant with their second child, was about to enter a potentially difficult labor. By the time Scott had eaten breakfast and received the morning ham radio call — a ritual he took a proprietary interest in since he often received news of his wife — it would be 10:00 A.M. or later before work started in the Gopher tent. One day Shoffner and Cardin watched in amazement as Scott spent an entire afternoon rigging a safety knot big enough to fill a bushel basket.

Among the improvements made to the Super Gopher III was a special nozzle designed to melt a six-inch hole to the plane. Then, instead of the two-inch guide pipe used the previous year, a four-inch pipe and a bilge pump were to be lowered so the meltwater around the Gopher could be pumped out as they went, increasing its efficiency. But the nozzle had been lost in transit, as had the antifreeze that was supposed to be added to the system. Word had it that the missing equipment was on

Gordon Scott takes the morning radio call.

Members of the 1992 expedition gather around the Super Gopher III for a group shot.

its way, although no one could swear to it. Cardin wanted to improvise using the old two-inch guidance system but Scott — with the support of Estes — elected to postpone operations. When Cardin pressed him, Scott would just say in his laconic way, "Nah, we need tuh wait another day."

That frustrated Cardin. As far as he was concerned, the old "summer camp for the boys" ethos was undermining the project. But Scott was in charge of the hole, and Cardin didn't feel he was in a position to overrule him. While acknowledging

Scott's many attributes, Cardin described him as a "rugged individualist who runs on his own time and isn't a good team player." To Cardin it seemed that consciously or unconsciously GES — as represented by Scott and Estes — didn't really care if they got an airplane or not. The search had sustained itself year after year because everyone had convinced themselves that even if they were unsuccessful, they'd come back again the following year, bankrolled mainly by someone else's money. As Cardin would later say, "I give 'em credit for the early years, but there comes a time when the old attitudes don't work anymore. You gotta finish dreaming and experimenting and just do it."

Scott thought Cardin was a pain in the ass, a typical military type barking orders and trying to take his and Estes's orderly operation and tune it to a crisis-level pitch. To Scott, Cardin was an interloper trying to apply urban America's frantic work ethic in an unwelcoming environment. Furthermore, Scott felt his background in alpine rescue and commercial fishing qualified him to judge what was safe around the Gopher hole, and he viewed Cardin's impatience as potentially dangerous. Besides, Scott didn't consider himself inflexible. When the six-inch pipe and the antifreeze still hadn't arrived after nearly a week, he agreed to use the two-inch pipe.

Despite that compromise, the operation progressed slowly through the rest of May. Some delays were unavoidable. More storms hit the camp, leaving waist-deep snowdrifts that forced most of the expeditioners to spend entire days digging out tents and equipment. Often neither the DC-3 nor a Dornier ski-plane Epps had rented could reach the site with supplies. At sixty-two feet the Super Gopher hit an obstruction — plywood and tarpaulin from the 1983 Winston Recovery Team expedition — that had to be removed. But it was a broken pump that focused attention sharply on Scott.

One day the chains and cables running to the Gopher and the pump became tangled, and the pump stopped working, bringing the entire operation to a halt. Both Scott and Estes tried to fix it in the hole, but without success. It seemed to be an electrical problem, but it was unclear whether the malfunction was in the pump's internal circuitry, in the power line that ran down the shaft or in the generator on the surface. Both men would later describe the incident as a difficult technical snafu that was complicated by the lack of appropriate tools and parts. But Shoffner and Cardin were frustrated by the length of time it took Scott to organize the initial visual inspection of the pump, and by his methodical, seemingly endless preparations before he or anyone else was allowed down the shaft. To them, the pump symbolized everything that was going wrong with Scott's leadership.

Even though the good-natured Shoffner was financing the project, he considered his presence on the ice cap that of an interested tourist with no authority over the operation. But he couldn't help worrying about what he saw as unnecessary holdups and late-starting workdays. Although his contract with GES stipulated the recovery of three planes, it was nearing the end of May and the Gopher was a little more than halfway to the first one. Since he knew that most of the crew's contracts ended toward the end of July, it didn't take much figuring to conclude that the expedition was going to be lucky to recover one plane that summer. He admired Scott, but he felt that GES's most experienced, resourceful and, at $5,000 per month, highest-paid crew member was turning into a liability. Still, it was up to Epps or Cardin to deal with Scott, even though neither seemed to be having much success.

Although Epps mainly flew sorties back and forth between Kulusuk and the camp, whenever he stayed on the ice cap he shared a tent with Cardin and Shoffner. One night, with the pump problem unresolved, Shoffner told Epps that Scott was running things at a turtle's pace. Epps, who was flying out again the next day, admitted that he was tired of trying to make Scott change.

"Roy," he said, "I've done all I can do. You've got the gold, you're in charge. Do what you want to do."

Shoffner agreed to talk to Scott. "If he doesn't give me some kind of affirmative plan of action, he's gonna pack his bags and get on the next plane out of here."

The next morning Shoffner met Scott outside the mess tent. "I've got something I want to talk to you about," he said. "Things are going to have to change. We've got to get moving — we're not making any progress."

To Shoffner's relief, a cheerful Scott acknowledged that things weren't moving as quickly as they should and he enthusiastically outlined his plans for resolving the pump problem and melting directly to the plane.

At 5:00 A.M. on Sunday, May 31, around the time Scott had estimated the Gopher should reach the plane, an excited Shoffner awoke and walked over to the Gopher tent. "Hey, Roy," Scott said, "measure down and tell me how far the Gopher is."

Peering down the hole, Shoffner let the measuring tape fall. Turning to Scott, he said, "Two hundred and fifty-seven feet."

A few minutes later Scott asked Shoffner to throw the tape down again to measure the Gopher's progress. Shoffner unraveled the measuring tape a second time. "It's still two hundred and fifty-seven feet," he said. "What's that mean?"

Scott's poker face stared back at Shoffner. "What does that mean, Roy?"

A triumphant grin crossed Shoffner's face as Scott told him that engine oil mixed with the water being pumped up could mean only one thing — the Gopher was sitting on top of some part of the plane. Shoffner congratulated Scott and the three men working with him on the night shift, and they signed their names in the Gopher logbook below Scott's entry that read, "BINGO! P-38." Then one of the men got the hunting rifle stored in the mess tent and fired a round into the air, awakening the camp.

Everyone was happy, but there wasn't the jubilation of 1989, when they'd brought up a piece of a plane, or 1990, when the Gopher had come to rest on *Big Stoop*. Ten minutes later, when Estes arrived, Scott said, "Guess we know how to do this now, 'cause we just did it again." There was, as Estes put it, "more a sense of relief that we were finally there, and now the real work was to come."

With the Gopher left to cook for the rest of the day, most of the crew used the time to shore up their tents, wash clothing or perform odd jobs around the camp. That night Epps, aware that morale had been low, tried to rouse the troops by giving an inspirational address. He talked about GES's history and the constant financial pressures leading up to the '92 expedition. Toward the end, just when it seemed that he had defused the tensions and boosted

In the excitement of the discovery, however, old conflicts were temporarily forgotten. A few days later Shoffner was dressed from head to toe in rain gear and strapped into a bosun's chair waiting to make his first descent to the P-38 when he heard the sound of an approaching plane's engines. He waited until Epps had landed and suited up. "I think Pat should be the first to go down," Shoffner told Scott. "And I'll be about three feet behind him."

On the way down, Epps fretted about the condition of the plane and wondered whether his hopes were going to be dashed again. When he reached the bottom, he could see that the Gopher had melted a cavern exposing part of the wing and the tip of one prop, all of the cockpit and the nose of the plane all the way to the tips of the machine guns. He was elated. The metal was dented in places but nothing appeared to be badly damaged, let alone crushed like the B-17.

Gordon Scott prepares for a descent into the Gopher hole.

everyone's spirits, he reaffirmed that Scott was in charge of the Super Gopher operation and Cardin of the camp. It was a compromise. Epps avoided the potential for additional discord that might have developed had he put Cardin in overall command, thereby "demoting" Scott. But it surprised Shoffner and especially Cardin, who realized that the announcement reinforced Scott at his expense.

That answered the question that had haunted him for eleven years. Clambering carefully over the slippery surface of the wing to where Shoffner had seated himself in the P-38's cockpit, Epps said, "Congratulations, Roy."

"Well, it's awfully good to get this far," Shoffner said, and both men laughed heartily. They agreed the plane was salvageable, and shook hands on it.

(Overleaf) A member of the GES is about to be winched down through 250 feet of icy Gopher shaft.

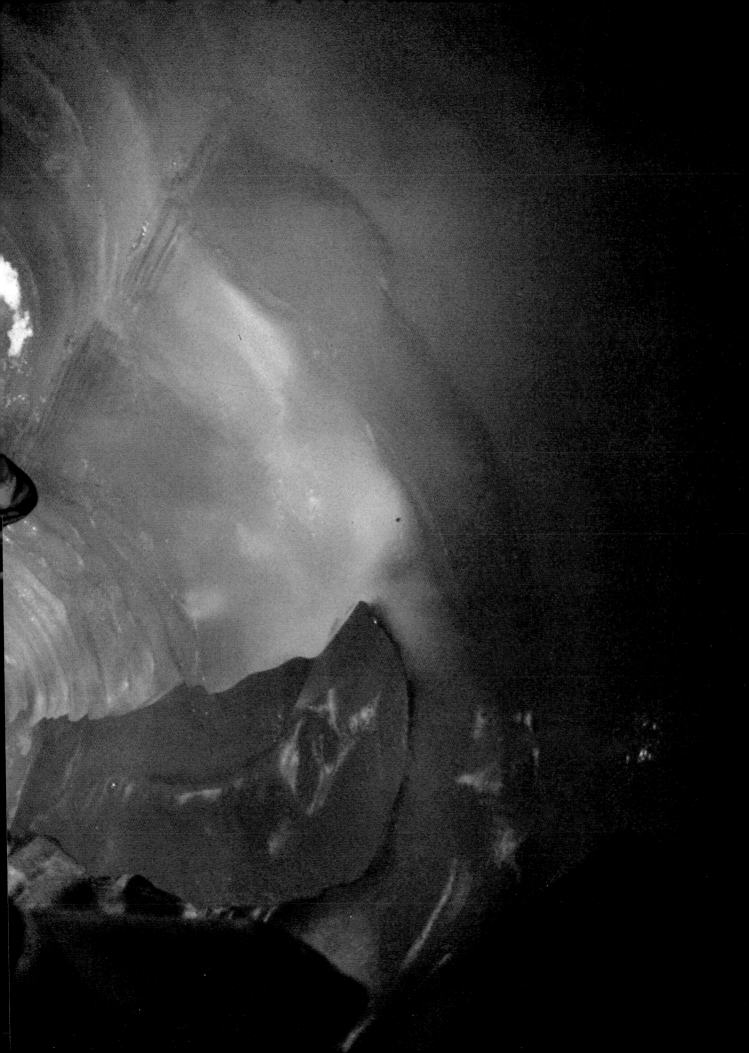

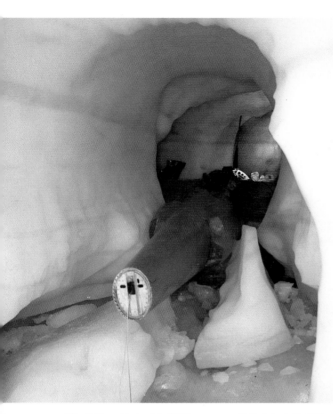

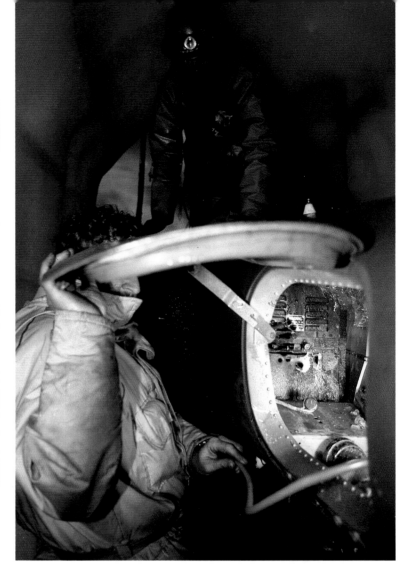

The P-38 uncovered in 1992 was essentially intact. But fifty years in a glacier had made an impact. The tail had come free from the rest of the plane (above and below). Working on it (right) required burrowing a separate cave a few feet behind the rest of the plane (opposite).

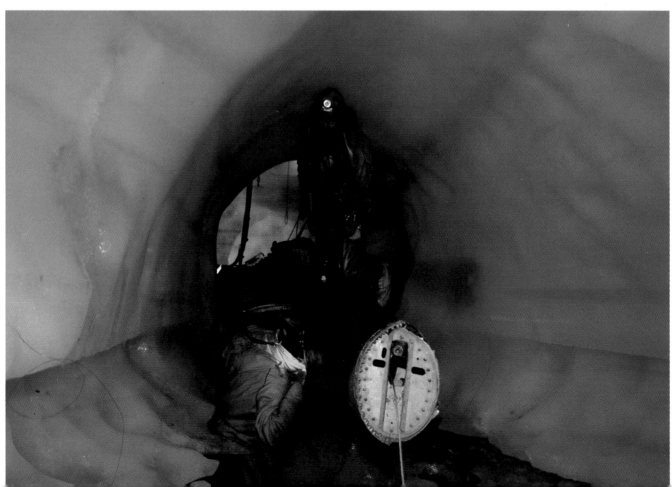

Looking at the P-38's sleek nose, with its cannon and machine guns, rusted but still in place, the mystique of the legendary fighter is easy to understand.

While the aircraft had been badly battered, unlike Big Stoop it was still basically intact. The classic fork-tailed profile of the P-38 (inset above) is readily evident here. The work of taking it apart has begun and it almost looks like these partially completed Lightnings in the Lockheed plant. (inset below).

Fifty years inside a glacier have smashed the Plexiglas in the pilot's canopy, but otherwise the cockpit looks much as it did fifty years ago.

Gordon Scott works at the hub of one of the propellers, trying to loosen blades still frozen into the ice.

ON SUNDAY, JUNE 14, DAVE KAUFMAN carefully picked his way around the P-38, helping Lou Sapienza photograph the plane. They had lowered what seemed like several hundred pounds of Sapienza's camera and lighting equipment down the hole, and while Sapienza set up the lights, Gordon Scott chiseled out a larger area in front of the plane's nose for the photographer to stand in. Each time Scott's chisel struck, it made a frighteningly explosive pop, and cracks shot across the width of the cavern. Although Kaufman had been working in the hole along with the others for two weeks, he still jumped when he heard the sounds and stared uneasily at the deep fissures that scored the cavern's roof.

The entire plane was exposed, cast in the eerie glow of halogen lights. On the top of the left wing was the insignia used by the U.S. Army Air Force early in the war. On the underside of the right wing there was another insignia and the word "U.S." The cramped cockpit was in remarkable condition, its gauges and instruments intact. The Lightning's trademark twin tail booms disappeared into a pair of ice tunnels that

opened into a second small cavern containing the tail section, which had been wrenched from the booms but sat in place, supported by the ice.

Epps was back in the U.S. picking up two mechanics from California who were going to dismantle the plane, so Sapienza spent ten hours recording it from every angle. In his most arresting photo, taken from in front of the nose, Kaufman is kneeling at the rear of the left boom while Scott can be seen rappelling from the Gopher shaft onto the right engine.

Scott and Kaufman decided to make the evening radio broadcast from the hole. "This is P-38 Delta, number 17630," Scott said, speaking into the hand-held walkie-talkie. "Gordon in the cockpit and Dave and Lou on the wings."

On the surface, someone held the second walkie-talkie up to the ham radio. Ernie Bracy, a retired air traffic controller who operated a ham radio station in Maine and was in contact with the ice cap twice a day, radioed, "I suggest you de-ice the aircraft before taking off."

"All ice has been removed from the wings," Scott said, to which Bracy replied, "You are cleared to fly." Scott ended the conversation by informing Bracy that their battery was going dead.

The next day, Bracy was told that Scott had been using the fifty-year-old battery in the P-38, which still carried a charge. What began as a prank turned into an international hoax as an excited Bracy reported the extraordinary news across a network that included ham radio stations in North America, Britain and Europe. While Bracy repeatedly asked for the make, model and voltage of the battery, newspaper and magazine articles were reporting that when the ignition was activated, the battery contained sufficient power to light up the instrument panel. Kaufman was disgusted that Bracy had been misled, and he was concerned that GES's credibility would be undermined by such childish behavior.

On June 30 Epps returned in the DC-3 with the mechanics, Gary Larkins and Thomas "T. K." Mohr. Larkins and Mohr were restoration experts who specialized in recovering warbirds from ocean bottoms and jungles. Neither man was a stranger to discomfort; Larkins, for example, had just returned from New Guinea, where he had waded in six inches of swamp water while dismantling a vintage fighter in temperatures that hit 115 degrees, sleeping at night on the wreck's wing because of the snakes swarming in the elephant grass below. Nonetheless, when he first stood at the bottom of the Gopher shaft and Epps asked him what he thought, he said, "I've been

around the world three times but I ain't never seen nothing like this before."

Soon Larkins and Mohr were soaked from lying in near-freezing pools of water trying to reach engine hoses, lines and bolts. One day Larkins struggled to remove a radiator scoop. Normally he could reach into the scoop with a stubby screwdriver and remove a series of small screws that attached it to the tail boom, but the scoop was crushed. Instead he chipped away at a block of ice inside the tail boom, then rigged a chisel to an extension and tried to knock the nuts off from the other side. An hour later the scoop fell into his hands. As Larkins inspected the radiator he noticed something drawn on the primer paint. When he brought a lamp closer, he saw a crude caricature of a Japanese face with huge ears. Clearly inspired by the wartime phrase "Loose lips sink ships," it had been signed by two workers assembling the P-38 in Lockheed's Burbank, California, factory in 1942. It was one of those tiny human touches that can reach across half a century.

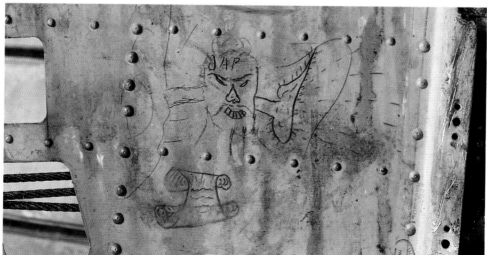

When restoration expert Gary Larkins pried off an air scoop, he found this crude drawing done by a worker at Lockheed fifty years ago, warning of the danger of loose talk.

Cold Mining

Salvaging the P-38 from the glacier took hard work, all of which had to be performed in cramped surroundings in a rain of melting water and chunks of ice that periodically fell from the cavern roof. First, the cavern had to be made large enough to work in and all parts of the plane freed from the ice. Then (below right) experts had to disassemble the plane, an arduous process that frequently meant prying apart pieces frozen together for decades. Finally (below center) the plane's individual parts had to be hauled to the surface, a trip equal to hauling them up the side of a tall building.

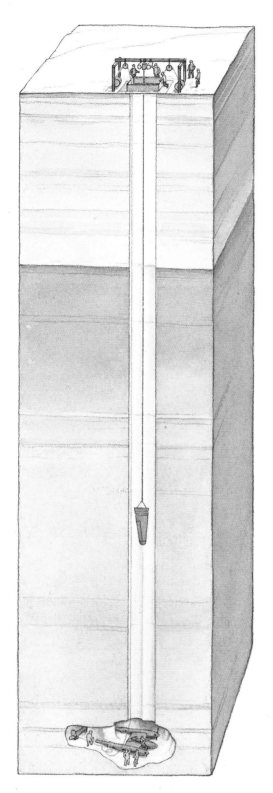

Once the parts of the plane had been pulled to the surface (left), they had to be manhandled out of the hole (below and bottom, left to right), an arduous job that was accomplished largely by hand. (Right) The P-38's wing rests on the summer snow together with the nose.

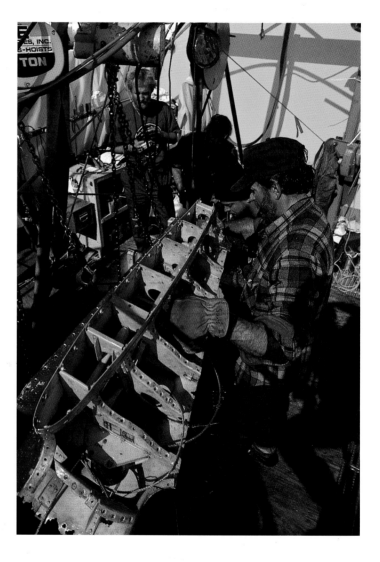

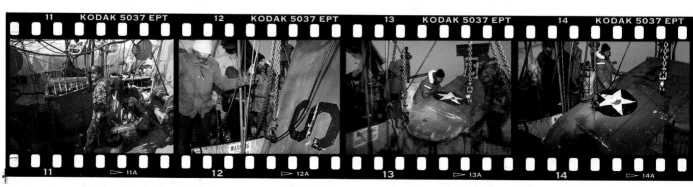

(Top) Souvenirs from the salvaged P-38. On the left is a tobacco tin. On the right is emergency oxygen equipment.
(Above) Gordon Scott and David Kaufman pose with the 20-mm cannon from the P-38. (Opposite) The gun and its ammo drum.

Fifty years to the day the Lost Squadron went down, a ceremony was held on the ice cap to mark the event. Oran Earl Toole, who had been a member of the party sent to bring out the downed flyers, reads a tribute to the airmen and the men who rescued them.

By mid-July Larkins and Mohr were gone, and an impressive collection of P-38 hardware was on the surface, including both wings, both engines, both booms and the tail section, all of which were moved around the site using the recovered Pizzagalli bulldozer. Smaller treasures included a set of keys found on the cockpit floor behind the throttle quadrant, the instrument panel, ammunition canisters, .50-caliber shells, smoke grenades, assorted tools, an oxygen bail-out bottle, a brass and wood antenna, a sealed fifty-year-old package of tobacco, a Lockheed manual and a checklist, on which pilot Harry Smith's writing was still legible. Meanwhile, three more Gopher shafts had been sunk and a fourth was under way in an effort to widen the hole

sufficiently to bring up the massive center section of the plane.

At 11:40 A.M. on Wednesday, July 15, fifty years to the moment that Brad McManus had touched down on the ice cap, the expedition members gathered. The two outer wing panels of the P-38 stood on their leading edge in the snow, forming a backdrop for the nose section with its four .50-caliber machine guns and 20-mm cannon still in place. Richard Taylor, who had returned to attend the ceremony, gave his customary "dreamers of the day" introduction. Then Epps recapped GES's history and thanked everyone who had contributed. He was followed by the guest of honor, seventy-four-year-old Brad McManus, who described how after surviving his wheels-down landing, he'd seen his colleague, Harry Smith, whose plane now sat in fragments on the ice cap, and the other pilots glide in to join him. It was an emotional moment for McManus, whose eyes teared and voice broke as he talked about what it meant for him to return to the ice cap.

The next speaker was Earl Toole, the radio operator who had been on Fred Crockett's rescue mission. After Toole read a tribute to all of the downed fliers and the rescue team, Don Brooks, Dan Callahan and Roy Shoffner said a few words. Then Epps started everyone singing "America the Beautiful," but no one could remember the words. Finally the Lightning's 20-mm cannon was lashed to the snowmobile, loaded with a half-century-old high-explosive round and fired at a 55-gallon fuel drum. The impact flipped the drum over as though it was a beer can.

The ceremony's goodwill, however, was at odds with the tensions that lay beneath the surface of the camp. In the early years, the expeditions had been camping trips in the snow for a few good ol' southern boys. But once they'd located the planes with radar and perfected the Super Gopher as a way to

melt through the ice cap, the project evolved into less of a summer adventure and more of a professional engineering operation. In the summer of 1992, with the technology, manpower and funding finally in place, the transition was complete. An impossible dream had turned into an achievable goal.

GES's past was upheld by Taylor, Scott, Estes and one or two others. Reflecting back on 1992 a year later, Estes said, "At some point things went downhill. Shoffner and his crew changed the perception of the expedition and GES lost control. All the work, the failures and successes of past expeditions were forgotten, the spirit of grand adventure gone. The attitude was just to get an airplane up, and when it's up the job's done."

Lightning pilot Brad McManus holds the nose of the P-38. For the ceremony's climax, the 20mm cannon was (below left to right) strapped to a snowmobile and fired at an oil drum, with spectacular results.

Shoffner and Cardin, however, came to see their role as the expedition's future. As Cardin said, "Believe you me, I like to have fun, but if somebody tells me to get an airplane out I'm gonna do whatever it takes to do that."

Despite Cardin's efforts to enact changes, Scott remained in control of the Gopher tent, with Estes's loyal support. For safety reasons Scott rarely permitted more than two people to accompany him to the plane, which had slowed excavating the cavern throughout June. Finally, when Epps arrived with the mechanics, he overruled Scott and ordered a team down the hole. Even taking into account that tensions are magnified any time a group of people work side by side at a remote location, a surprised Epps listened to complaints about Scott not only from Cardin, who was ready to quit the expedition, but also from Kaufman and other hard-working members of the crew. They said Scott was difficult and inflexible, refused to entertain alternatives or take any shortcuts to speed the process. Epps was even more surprised to hear that Neil Estes, who worked closely with Scott, had become moody and negative in his outlook. Estes had been the most vocal critic of the poor planning and lack of tools, and sometimes his presence was enough to empty the mess tent. His favorite phrase, parroted behind his back by the others, was "It can't be done."

Evaluating their progress, Epps and Brooks were forced to admit that things were getting out of control. Sapienza, who was embroiled in a dispute with GES about past expenses and photo rights, had all but abandoned his cooking duties even though he'd been hired to do the job at $3,000 per month. In a noisy confrontation, Epps fired him. But Scott was a touchier issue. He had been part of every expedition since 1986, and he knew more about surviving in arctic conditions than the rest of them combined. In consideration of their friend's experience and seniority, Epps and Brooks — with Taylor's assent — had put him in charge. Sadly, they realized that they should have brought him to the ice cap only long enough to locate the planes and get the operation set up. He had to go, and the one to tell him wasn't going to be the soft-spoken, nonconfrontational Brooks.

Epps took Scott aside and said, "Gordon, you're going home on Friday. We're running out of money."

Scott was stunned, but he took it so stoically it was hard to tell. It was all about politics, of that he was sure, and it involved his unwillingness to march to Cardin's military beat. And since Epps had said it was about money even though Scott saw no sign of financial problems, he figured Shoffner might be involved as well.

Flying back to the U.S. with Taylor, Scott said, "Richard, I've never been fired before. Tell me what happened."

At first Taylor tried to deflect his friend's question. Then he explained that the consensus had been that Scott wasn't committed to bringing an aircraft up, that he was working at a relaxed pace, enjoying a summer job.

"I can have a summer job that's a lot easier and more comfortable and more fun than this," Scott said. During a stopover in Goose Bay, he pressed the issue, and Taylor admitted that Epps and Shoffner felt that he wasn't a team player. Maybe there's something to that, Scott conceded. The next day, in Bangor, Maine, Taylor told Scott that he'd been thinking, and that maybe the problem wasn't about being a team player, but about his reaction to leadership. When the leadership is smart and strong, Taylor elaborated, everything runs smoothly. When it's weak or there's bullshit, you react strongly.

Was that a comment on his leadership or Cardin's, Scott wondered. He returned to Alaska feeling alternately confused and betrayed.

On the ice cap, meanwhile, another decision was dividing GES and Shoffner. Epps and Brooks were ferrying loads of P-38 parts to Kulusuk, where they intended to pack the DC-3 with as much as it would carry and fly to Oshkosh, Wisconsin, to attend the Experimental Aircraft Association's annual air show that began July 30. GES had rented a prime location with the promise that they would be exhibiting parts of the first Lost Squadron plane to be resurrected from its icy tomb.

Weeks earlier Shoffner had said that while the decision was theirs, he couldn't understand why they'd want to show off a collection of bent-up parts rather than continue the program on the ice cap. "You've got tents, equipment and people already up there," he told Epps. "For $50,000 we could melt a single hole to another P-38 to

To remove the center section of the P-38, the largest part of the plane, several Gopher holes had to be combined into one large hole big enough for the section.

the international media. It was a chance to make a publicity splash, to sell a lot of t-shirts, caps and pins, and to focus attention on the successful recovery of the plane. With Epps and Brooks wondering where they were going to come up with the money to split the shipping and restoration costs with Shoffner, Oshkosh seemed like a perfect opportunity to advertise their investment potential. As Epps put it, "If Shoffner can't understand that, it's because he already has money."

There was still the problem of getting the last and largest part of the plane up. From the beginning, the Gopher's frame and its winches had been barely adequate for hoisting the larger parts of the Lightning to the surface. Now they were after the center section, which measured seventeen feet by twenty-one feet and weighed two tons. Epps and

determine whether it's worth coming back another year. If you wait, it'll cost $250,000 to mount another expedition."

But Epps and Brooks felt that the benefits of leaving outweighed those of staying. Oshkosh was one of the aviation world's biggest events, a magnet for aviation buffs from all over North America as well as

Kaufman had traveled to Kulusuk and come up with a twenty-foot-long 1,200-pound steel beam to add heft to the frame, and by excavating the 1990 Pizzagalli and GES storage tents, they'd retrieved several winches to add lifting power. But even if they managed to hoist the center section out of the hole, getting it back to the U.S.

was another question. They'd received word confirming that it was too big to fit inside either a C-130 or C-141, and military officials were doubtful they could send anything larger. In any event, since it was clear that the center section could not be removed and shipped to the U.S. in time for Oshkosh, Shoffner offered to stay in order to allow Epps to go.

On Thursday, July 23, after several days had been spent enlarging the four Gopher holes into one large shaft, the center section was turned on its side and shifted into position, a task made all the harder now that more than half of the crew's contracts were up, and many had left the ice cap. A $\frac{3}{4}$-inch steel cable was threaded through an eye hook located where the uppermost engine nacelle met the spar. Then the cable was secured to a similar hook on the second engine nacelle below it, so the structure was being hoisted from the bottom. The cable ran up the shaft to a powerful grip hoist that was to provide most of the lift. A pair of 4,000-pound hand-operated winches were attached to the engine mount and a wheel-well nacelle, while two 1-ton electric chain hoists, their chains secured to either side of the center section, were used for delicate maneuvering. By Sunday evening, with Wee Gee Smith riding shotgun, using his body weight to shift the fuselage past some obstructions and chipping and melting away the larger ones, the truncated aircraft inched its way above the 200-foot level.

The next morning Epps and Brooks departed with half a dozen of the remaining crew who had commitments back home. Although they were uncomfortable leaving before the center section was safely out, both

With only inches to spare, the center section of the P-38 is winched up the enlarged shaft.

(Above) Attached to the plane were cables that ran up to several winches. (Center) The bulk of the lifting was done by one very powerful manually operated hoist. Using it required applying great pressure uniformly, and only ex-Green beret Sam Knaub had the necessary strength. (Right) Several people on the surface were needed to monitor the various winches, and someone had to ride on the plane to make sure it came up evenly and to help it around any obstacles in the shaft.

men convinced themselves they'd left it in good hands.

As the DC-3 disappeared into the distance, psychological shock descended on the camp. Shoffner wasn't so much angry as perplexed. He couldn't understand how, after eleven years of hardship and expense, Epps could leave when the largest and most difficult piece of the plane was dangling less than a third of the way up the shaft.

Cardin, on the other hand, was appalled. The purpose of the expedition had been to get three planes, and now Epps was leaving before they'd recovered one. Since Cardin was in charge of the operation, he also felt abandoned. Neil Estes, who had turned into a real asset once Scott was gone, had flown back to Atlanta. And the dependable Wee Gee Smith was also gone.

In fact, only seven people remained to finish bringing the center section out of the hole. Aside from Shoffner and his wife, Eddie Lou, who was cooking the meals, the crew consisted of Iceman Frostason; Sam Knaub, an ex-Green Beret who knew

Don Brooks; John Fugedy, an engineer and pilot; and Jorn Skyrud, a young Norwegian pilot who'd offered his services to Epps at the beginning of the summer. With the exception of Knaub, a bodybuilder and former paratrooper, it wasn't exactly Cardin's idea of an all-star team, but at least everyone was enthusiastic and there were no prima donnas.

The biggest problem was the manually operated grip hoist, which carried the weight of the plane and required eighty pounds of pressure to move the handle. When the handle was raised, the cable came up a quarter of an inch. When it was lowered, the cable moved another quarter of an inch, so for every four pumps the center section rose an inch. Although Cardin, Fugedy, Frostason and Skyrud were able to pump it, they continually broke shear pins. Only the powerfully built Knaub was strong enough to apply an even amount of pressure and feel the subtle changes in the cable's tension.

So Knaub manned the main hoist while Cardin, Fugedy and Frostason took turns on the hand winches, Shoffner acted as a spotter and Skyrud rode up on the plane, calling instructions into a hand-held radio. When it was necessary to shift the section through a tight part of the shaft, Skyrud would say, "Up on red" or "Up on yellow," referring to the color-coded electric winches controlled by Eddie Lou, who held a red and yellow button in either hand. It was exhausting work easing it up in such tiny increments, carefully monitoring all systems, fearful that any failure might send the beast plummeting to the bottom of the shaft, where it would be utterly destroyed.

When the section reached eighty feet, it could be seen from the surface, which created a new problem. Every time Skyrud had to maneuver around a tricky part of the shaft, everyone had an opinion. After

watching Skyrud being second-guessed for a while, Cardin said, "Hold it. Jorn's on the plane, he's in charge. Will everybody please shut up!"

On Friday, July 31, with the plane sixteen feet from the surface, the cable was so short that it lost any spring it had had, and the frame was becoming shaky. In order to reinforce it further, the ends of an enormous 5,000-pound strap used by the military for slinging equipment underneath aircraft were wrapped around a pair of 25-gallon fuel drums, which were filled with water and buried. Then the strap was secured to either side of the frame, firmly bracing it. Finally the crew spent the afternoon digging a gently angled six-foot ramp so the plane could slide out of the hole more easily. In the midst of all the work, Epps contacted

(Below) Once the center section had been winched to the surface, the crew had to dig away a ramp on one side onto which the plane could be pulled.

Finally, the center section of the plane was pulled out sideways onto the ice cap. The hardest single part of the excavation was over.

the camp from Oshkosh and was told the center section was at sixteen feet and would likely be removed the next day.

The next morning, under bright, sunny skies, the plane was raised until the top hook was at eye level. Then, after tightening the secondary winches to ease some of the tension on the cable, the top hook was removed. While Knaub used the main hoist to slowly raise it higher, Cardin released the pressure on the winches supporting the top, which allowed the bulky structure to fall forward onto a piece of plywood covering the ramp. Then they buried two more barrels and used attached straps to pull the piece clear of the hole.

When it lay flat on the ice cap, Cardin glanced at his watch: 4:23 P.M. "Well," he said, "we're officially out of the hole now."

With everyone gathered around the center section and Shoffner sitting in the cockpit, Cardin produced a bottle of champagne, which they all shared. While Eddie Lou videotaped the scene, the six men cheered lustily and toasted their accomplishment. When the bottle was empty, they signed it and dropped it down the Gopher shaft.

W HEN SHOFFNER AND EDDIE LOU LEFT on August 3, Cardin and the rest of the crew dismantled the camp, moving everything that was being left behind to an area next to the closest P-38, in preparation for a future expedition. A thirty-foot steel pipe was attached to a 55-gallon fuel drum as a marker.

By the middle of August, Fugedy had gone to Sondre Stromfjord to arrange for the cargo to be shipped back to the States, and Frostason and Skyrud were on their way home. Cardin and Knaub were picked up by a Bell 212 helicopter and flown to the ice cap where they were met by a Sikorsky S-61, a heavy-duty cargo copter that was to lift the center section. The first time the chopper's pilot tried to lift it, he succeeded in dragging it only about a foot off the ground for thirty feet. Then he landed and jettisoned some tools and other heavy gear while Cardin shortened the sling by twelve feet so the copter would be operating closer to ground effect — an aeronautical phenomenon in which aircraft experience greater lift. By then the air had cooled a little and the wind had picked up. Cardin didn't know which combination of factors made the difference, but the copter lifted the center section easily and carried it to Kulusuk.

Two weeks later the section was loaded onto a Danish ship that carried it to Denmark, and from there it was shipped to Sweden where a freighter picked it up and delivered it to the docks at Savannah, Georgia.

Epps hadn't wanted to undertake the restoration at Epps Aviation, so he and Brooks suggested that Shoffner take it to his hangar in Middlesboro. Aside from the fact that they couldn't think of anywhere else to put it, Epps and Brooks thought that since Shoffner had put up the $350,000 for the expedition, plus an additional $75,000 in overruns (which rose to nearly $100,000 when the shipping charges were included), it was only fair that they demonstrate their good faith by letting him store the aircraft. It would give him confidence that his

The center section of the P-38 being flown by helicopter to the coast.

investment was protected, they reasoned, and Shoffner was willing to start the restoration by spending his share of the costs while they raised their share.

SIX MONTHS LATER, ON FRIDAY, APRIL 30, 1993, Epps, Brooks, Bobbie Bailey and several visitors milled about in Shoffner's hangar in Middlesboro. "Glacier Girl," as Harry Smith's P-38 had been named, was in pieces, some of it scattered around the floor, the rest of it stored on huge shelving units against the back wall. Only a pair of steel spars, extending nearly the width of the hangar from either side of a steel beam, provided a skeletal suggestion of the plane that was to come. Two restoration specialists hired by Shoffner were bent over work tables, one of them hammering out dented metal parts and the other one measuring and cutting large sheets of aluminum and drilling holes in them. The hangar resounded with the shrill whine of a power drill and the repeated whack of a hammer.

Shoffner explained the process of restoring original parts and having replacements made following Lockheed's original specifications. He stopped beside a table on which the control column sat.

"There's two little pieces in there, Pat," he said, turning to Epps. "When you turned this friction lock they cramped up against the throttle. They're made out of naval brass, not an inch long and they're about three-eighths of an inch thick on this end, machined down to a quarter of an inch. One of them's broken, the other one's not. They were back inside of this column,

where nothing could get to 'em. But they were under the ice, so the expansion process got to 'em."

Epps smiled and shook his head. "Amazing," he said.

Restoring the plane was beginning to seem like the easiest part of the expedition's aftermath. As of April, Shoffner had spent nearly $1 million on the expedition, transportation and restoration costs. GES still hadn't paid him for its share of the restoration or contributed toward the overruns that Shoffner had covered when the expedition exceeded its budget late in the summer. Bailey had agreed to finance GES's share, but there were many disputes over the three-page contract between GES and Shoffner, which, among other things, covered the merchandise, book, film and video rights that Bailey believed were hers. There was also a debate about whether to sell the plane for top dollar on the open market — which Epps estimated to be as high as $3 million but Shoffner insisted would be under $2 million — or agree to let Shoffner buy it through a complicated process that would retire GES's debts. Clearly there was a lot of sorting out to be done, which would happen slowly, over time, with the help of costly lawyers. Considering GES's history of financial woes, these postpartum blues seemed predictable, if not inevitable.

Yet for two hours on a sunny April morning, all that was forgotten as Epps, Brooks and Bailey felt the shivers of excitement that came whenever they touched an original part of the plane or stared at pilot Harry Smith's tobacco can. For Epps, searching for the Lost Squadron had never been a business venture. It had started as a romantic adventure, a chance for him and Taylor to become explorers and leave civilization behind. The challenge was in seducing the ice cap to give up its treasure. That done, the adventure came to an end as the plane was returned to the U.S., where it reentered the world of commerce and contracts.

"You just have to dig through it and solve it," Epps said later. "I don't like it, but I keep trying to solve the problem rather than bitchin'."

As for going back to recover more planes, Epps laughed and shook his head, pointing out that GES and Shoffner had brought back the first, and therefore most celebrated, of the aircraft: "Anything else is just economics. If a man wants one of those P-38s, we've proved it can be done."

One day, after eating at the Waffle House, a roadside diner that was a favorite of Epps's, he noticed a sign outside a church. It read, "Don't let yesterday take up too much of today." That's it, he told himself — that's what I'm trying to do.

In the hangar, the parts of the plane are spread out, and the hard task of restoration begins.

EPILOGUE

ON THE FINAL APPROACH TO THE TINY Middlesboro, Kentucky, airport, Pat Epps banked his twin-engine Piper Navajo until he was square with the runway, then began his descent, touching down a few moments later with a gentle thump. His passengers, Richard Taylor and Brad McManus, stared eagerly out the plane's windows searching for Roy Shoffner's hangar, hoping for their first glimpse of the P-38. But on this quiet Saturday morning in May 1994, the airport appeared to be deserted and the hangar was closed up as solidly as the Greenland ice cap. After taxiing to a halt, the men emerged from the Navajo and approached the hangar just as Shoffner and Bob Cardin pulled up in Shoffner's truck.

"Good morning, gentlemen," Shoffner said, shaking hands all around. As Cardin unlocked the door, Shoffner smiled at McManus and said, "Well, let's go on in."

The seventy-six-year-old McManus was wearing a navy blue baseball cap, striped sports shirt and beige trousers. His belt sported a large turquoise buckle. He looked like a rakish golf pro, but inside he felt a stirring of excitement that reminded him of his glory days as a World War II fighter jock. When he'd visited the ice cap

in the summer of 1992, McManus had seen a few pieces of the plane after they'd been hauled up the Gopher shaft. Now he was anxious to see it in its nearly restored state. From what he'd heard it was beginning to look like an airplane that would soon be flying for the first time in more than half a century.

Stepping inside the hangar, McManus was awestruck. The fuselage rested on stands made of wood and cement blocks, the wings supported by powerful jacks. Although the tail section, engines and landing gear were not yet in place — they were being rebuilt off-site — the aircraft was more than half assembled. Most of the newly fabricated metal surfaces were covered with a greenish yellow primer paint, chosen because it most closely matched the color of the zinc chromate used on the plane when it was manufactured in 1942. But a portion of the right boom, where McManus stood, was in its original state. The metal looked its age and the red, white and blue paint of the air force insignia had faded and blistered. McManus ran the palm of his hand lovingly across the surface as though he was stroking a cat.

"Feel this," he said. "It's so smooth. Every wrinkle is out of it. These babies were brand

The P-38 under reconstruction. The bullet-shaped objects festooning the plane are temporary fasteners used to keep parts in place while they are being worked on.

new airplanes when we flew them onto the ice cap. Over the years the ice twisted and dented that metal but you'd never know it."

McManus slowly walked around the wing, admiring the craftsmanship. Epps, Taylor and Shoffner joined him and together they inspected the fuselage.

"Isn't it nice?" asked Shoffner.

"Beautiful," McManus replied.

"Every nut, bolt and rivet is new," said Shoffner.

Epps pointed to a section of original metal below the cockpit that bore the name "H. L. Smith" in faded letters. "You've reused this skin, haven't you?"

Shoffner nodded. "Yeah. Anywhere we had a piece halfway good we tried to use it." Sweeping his hand toward the rest of the

plane, he added, "Most of this other's been replaced."

McManus stared reflectively at the stenciled letters. "This is Harry's plane," he said. "When I flipped over I could hear planes above me. After I crawled out and waved to let them know I was all right, I looked up and there was Harry rolling and looping this one."

Brad McManus, photographed on the ice cap in 1942 (right), examines the nose of the P-38 in May 1994 (below).

Someone asked McManus whether he remembered the first time he'd flown a P-38. McManus said he remembered it vividly. He'd been stationed at a naval base outside San Diego when he was a young cadet fresh out of flying school. "It used to be that they wouldn't put a kid in one of these unless he had about five hundred flying hours," McManus said. "The war changed that."

Peering inside the cockpit, McManus said: "There's the throttle, props, mixture control, all in place. It's exactly like it was when we climbed in 'em in '42. Probably better than when we got in 'em."

Standing at the nose, McManus examined the machine guns and 20-mm cannon. At this stage of reconstruction, every hole that would later contain a rivet or bolt was filled with temporary stoppers that resembled bullets and gave the plane an even more fearsome appearance than it already had. Taylor reminded McManus that the earliest P-38s had been equipped with more powerful 37-mm cannons. Why did Lockheed scale them down, Taylor asked.

"When you fired the 37-mm the plane stopped in midair," McManus said.

The men continued to admire the reconstruction and swap ice cap stories. At one point, a grinning Epps draped his arm over the broad shoulders of a smiling Shoffner. Everyone was relaxed and the mood was amiable even though a drama was being played out beneath the surface of events. Epps, Taylor and the rest of the Greenland Expedition Society still hadn't come up with their share of the restoration budget.

To date, Shoffner had paid for everything. If you included the 1992 expedition and all post-expedition costs, that amounted to well over a million dollars. Although *Glacier Girl* would fly, it was not clear who would eventually own her. At one point Epps drew Shoffner aside and handed him a sealed envelope. It was, he explained, a letter from Don Brooks outlining GES's latest financing scheme.

"Where is Don Brooks?" asked Cardin. "I expected him to be here today."

Epps told him that Brooks was busy painting the DC-3 in its World War II colors in preparation for the ceremonies commemorating the fiftieth anniversary of D-Day, taking place in England and France in a few weeks. Several hours before troops landed on the beaches on June 6, 1944, Brooks's plane, then part of the British air force, had dropped paratroopers behind enemy lines in the middle of the night, marking the beginning of the Normandy invasion. Now Brooks, accompanied by Epps, would fly to England where his plane was to be used to reenact that parachute drop. A group of D-Day veterans, most of them over seventy, were going to jump onto the same terrain they'd landed on fifty years ago.

"Did you take part in D-Day, Brad?" Cardin asked.

"My squadron was the first to move out over the fleet when it left port in southern England on June fifth," McManus replied. "At 3:30 the next morning, in a rainstorm, we flew cover for the fleet. Our orders were to intercept any enemy air activity, but I'd already flown to Berlin fourteen times, and to Hamburg, Munich and Dresden with B-17s and B-24s. By the time the D-Day invasion started, there was no German air force."

Ducking under the wing, Cardin asked McManus whether he remembered the story of Harry Smith shooting bullets into his electronic "Identification: Friend or Foe" transmitter.

"Yeah," McManus said. "Harry did that. Mine didn't need it because my plane was so damaged."

Cardin pointed to a pair of indentations in a piece of original metal on the boom. "This is where the bullets came through the IFF and hit the skin," he said.

The IFF, which was about the size of a carry-on suitcase, stood beneath the boom. There were several jagged holes through it. Cardin reached into the pocket of his jeans and removed a small, squashed piece of lead.

"This is one of the .45 slugs Harry used to shoot it," he told McManus. "It's shiny from jingling it with the pennies in my pocket."

"Son-of-a-gun!" said McManus.

Later, with everyone standing in a semicircle behind the plane next to a P-38 drop tank, McManus talked about the difficulties pilots encountered when flying aircraft overseas in the forties.

"The risk in that Bolero movement was that it was the first time they'd ever tried it," he said. "By today's standards, weather information and radio communications was crude beyond belief. We broadcast an SOS for three days without getting an answer."

"We tried that ourselves forty-five years later," Taylor said, thinking of his Golf Cart I escapade. "Now it only takes two days."

When the laughter died down, Epps turned to Shoffner and said, "Remember that beady snow, like ball bearings, that you couldn't shovel?"

Shoffner laughed heartily. "Anywhere there was a crack, it'd fill 'er up," he said. "The outhouse was full of snow every morning. In '92 that Gopher hut was eighteen feet wide by thirty feet long, and it was sunk into the snow. One night we had a storm with seventy mile-per-hour winds that filled the sucker right up."

The men reminisced about storms they'd weathered and tents that had collapsed. Then McManus said, "Bob and Roy, you should be commended for what you've accomplished here. It's fulfilled all my expectations to see how far along this plane has come in the dozen years since Pat and Richard began searching for it. To say nothing of the fifty-two years since we landed there."

To Epps, McManus said, "It's sure a long way from that first trip when you were going to fly 'em out, isn't it, Pat?"

Epps smiled. "All you gotta do is brush the snow off and fly 'em out," he said wistfully. "I remember Roy and I down there the first time, standing by the windshield of this plane. We'd melted maybe a third of the ice away and it looked good."

"We're probably lucky we couldn't see any more than we could, Pat," said Shoffner.

Later, McManus signed a bullet from the plane's original ammunition and posed for snapshots. Cardin handed him a plastic model of the P-38 and instructed him to hold it upside down.

"This is the way I remember it the last time I landed in Greenland," McManus said. "In fighter training they taught us to be positive and aggressive. I must have been extra positive and aggressive that day to try and land that plane with its wheels down."

After everyone had said their goodbyes, McManus stepped out of the hangar into the bright noonday sun. A dozen visitors who'd come to see the famous P-38 restoration waited patiently for the hangar to be opened.

"Say, folks," yelled Epps. "This here's Brad McManus. He flew one of the P-38s back in '42. He was the first one to land on the ice cap, the one that flipped over."

The crowd stared uncertainly at McManus,

the way people do when they learn that someone standing unrecognized among them is a movie star.

"You were really one of the P-38 pilots?" one man asked. Another said, "Do you mind if I take your picture?"

Surrounded by well-wishers eager to ask him about the crash-landing, take snapshots and collect his autograph, McManus enjoyed a few minutes basking in the warm glow of celebrityhood. As he walked slowly across the tarmac toward Epps's Navajo, he said, "I thought this story ended when we were rescued in 1942 but today it finally seemed like the end of a very long adventure."

Richard Taylor (left), author David Hayes, Brad McManus, Roy Shoffner, Bob Cardin(back to camera) and Pat Epps gather around the P-38.

Once the last part of the P-38 to be received, the large center section (right), was in Shoffner's hangar, work began on taking the plane apart (above).

As the plane was taken apart, each piece was carefully checked. Undamaged parts were cleaned while damaged ones were repaired or replaced. (Above) An expert works on the P-38's cockpit. Once the cockpit had been completely taken apart, this collection of parts (right) was the result.

Resurrecting a Warbird

"This airplane is special," said Bob Cardin. "We feel it's paramount that we return it to the exact same condition it was in when it left Lockheed's Burbank factory in 1942."

Cardin was explaining why he was having the P-38's turbosuperchargers rebuilt, even if the plane would never again fly high enough or fast enough to use them.

"If it had operational turbos when it left Burbank," Cardin said, "it's gonna have 'em when it leaves this hangar."

The restoration began on October 28, 1992, when all of the parts of the plane were finally gathered together in Roy Shoffner's hangar in Kentucky. Under Bob Cardin's supervision, warbird specialists started taking apart the plane's massive center section. They hoped that it might not need too much work. Unfortunately, the more they took the plane apart, the more damage they found, requiring still further

Ultimately (right) the cockpit would be reassembled, and then painted with primer. Before that, however, one of the first stages in rebuilding the plane was to reassemble the plane's center section (below right).

disassembly. Working systematically, part by part, they broke down the entire plane into its smallest manageable pieces, identifying each one with magic marker and placing it in one of many clearly labeled piles. Then each piece was cleaned and checked to see whether it could be used again, or would have to be repaired or replaced. In some cases, damaged parts served as templates to construct replacements.

To help with the restoration, Cardin began collecting an extensive research library. After Lockheed quoted him an exorbitant price for the technical drawings the company had in its archives, Cardin went instead to the Smithsonian Institution. For about $1,200, the Smithsonian supplied him with forty-eight reels of microfilm and numerous photocopies of World War II-era aviation maintenance handbooks, as well as P-38 parts and repair manuals. Between studying the plane itself and consulting the manuals, Cardin and his crew were able to more or less duplicate the original manufacturing process carried out during the 1940s.

In the spring of 1993, the crew began to rebuild the plane, using the main spar as a starting point. To make sure everything fit properly and no pieces were overlooked, each component was first attached using Clicos — temporary fasteners that resembled bullets. Once a part checked out, the crew bolted or riveted the piece into place.

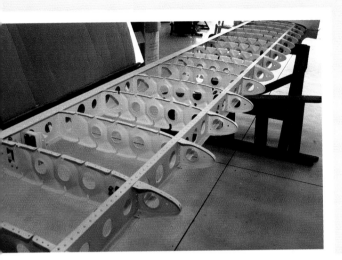

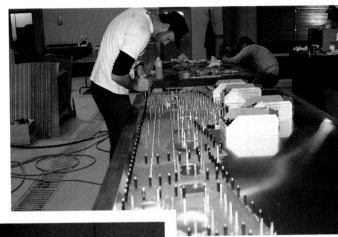

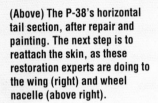

(Above) The P-38's horizontal tail section, after repair and painting. The next step is to reattach the skin, as these restoration experts are doing to the wing (right) and wheel nacelle (above right).

Acquiring existing parts was often cheaper than creating molds and building new ones from scratch, but finding them proved to be an adventure. More than once, Cardin and Shoffner visited people who claimed to have P-38s, only to discover a pile of scrap aluminum that most people wouldn't even have identified as an aircraft, let alone a Lightning. For a man who was supposed to be supervising a restoration, Cardin sometimes found himself spending more time playing amateur detective.

While searching for a nosewheel, he heard that a Buick dealer in Kansas City had a couple of them. After working the phones for several days, he tracked down the dealer, who agreed to donate one. Another

time, after spending months searching for a control yoke, Cardin found one only to learn that its owner was unwilling to part with it. He began calling contacts in the vintage aircraft world and following up on obscure tips until he eventually found a cache of two hundred in a warehouse whose owner hadn't realized what they were.

Cardin needed engine cowlings to replace the plane's badly crushed originals, but when he finally found a pair their owner was only interested in trading for a Wright 1820, a rare model of aircraft engine. Months later, Cardin located one, for which he had to trade another type of engine. Finally

(Right) By March of 1994, the P-38 was beginning to look like a plane again, with its twin booms back on and much of its aluminum outer skin in place. (Below) Although some surfaces were badly damaged, others were good enough to use again. (Below right) A shot of the nose and cockpit, now almost complete.

he was able to swap the Wright for the cowlings.

Many components were restored by companies donating their services or charging a nominal sum. For example, a plastics firm in Pennsylvania fabricated a duplicate canopy, and B. F. Goodrich Aerospace in England rebuilt the landing gear and brakes at no cost. An aviation mechanic volunteered to rebuild the plane's Allison engines for the cost of the parts, and an aviation electrician agreed to replace the wiring. In most cases, Cardin discovered, people were eager to contribute to so unique a project.

When work is completed, *Glacier Girl*, as the P-38 has been named, will be one of the most perfect warbird restorations ever. Many other restored warbirds consist of just a very few original parts, and a mish-mash of brand-new and adapted components. Not *Glacier Girl*. That's because the plane that crash-landed on the ice was virtually brand-new and built to very high standards.

"They changed a lot of the manufacturing processes on later models of P-38," said Cardin. "They were putting out sixteen a day in the heart of wartime production, and the realities of war made them disposable airplanes. The quality of craftsmanship was much higher on the early models, like this one.

"This is going to be the finest P-38 in the world, and it may be the finest restoration of any warbird ever done."

(Overleaf) The restored P-38, now dubbed Glacier Girl, as it will look in flight as envisioned by painter William S. Phillips.

ACKNOWLEDGMENTS

GES has been fortunate to have enjoyed the enthusiastic and dedicated support of a number of people and businesses. This support has been in the form of donated time, materials and money. The "Lightning Brigade" has over 1,000 members. Additional support has come from the hundreds of individuals who have purchased the GES merchandise. GES is grateful to all who have contributed to these seven expeditions — it has been a team effort.

GROUND SUPPORT

Ernie Bracy
Pat Cardin
Tom Deardorff
Jo Engle
Ann Epps
Ben T. Epps, Jr.
Elaine Epps
George Guerin

Suzanne Holly
Nancy Krewson
Kathi Parks
Bob Pope
O. Earl Toole
George Wald
George Wald, Sr.
Pat Wald

Julia Weaver
Lori White

HAM RADIO OPERATORS
Henry Barr
Leo G. Janssens
Don Lopez

SUPPORT AND CLOSE COOPERATION

Danish and Greenlandic
  Governments
The Greenlanders
Torbin Dahl and Kulusuk
  Base Personnel
Sondrestrom Base
  Personnel
USAF
109th Airlift Group, New
  York Air National Guard

Brooks Auto Parts
Epps Air Service, Inc.
Our-Way, Inc.
Pinnacle Airways, Inc.

A. O. Smith Water
  Products Co.
B. F. Goodrich
Marti Electronics, Inc.

Academy Airlines
Odin Air

Old Sarge — Tommy
  Smith
Athens Airport
Frederick Aviation
Lowe Aviation

Bausch & Lomb
Bose
LaCrosse Footwear, Inc.
Northern Outfitters
Snapper

GES EXPEDITIONS

I 1981 (August 1–9)
Roy Degan
Pat Epps
Russell Rajani
Richard Taylor

II 1981 (October 18–23)
Bruce Bevan
Pat Epps
Russell Rajani
Richard Taylor
Norman Vaughan

III   1986 (July 12–26)
Fred Agree
Bruce Bevan
Jud Chalmers
Roy Degan
Doug Epps
Pat Epps
Patrick Epps, Jr.
Susan Epps
Gordon Scott
Chuck Sutherland
Richard Taylor
Norman Vaughan

IV   1988 (July 10-July 29)
Helgi Bjoernsson
* Larry Bramon
Dan Callahan, M.D.
Pat Epps
Neil Estes
Steve Felker
Tom Foley
Addi Hermannsson
Austin Kovacs
Bill Marlow
C.W. Marlow
Gordon Scott

Jon Sveinsson
Richard Taylor
Bil Thuma
Norman Vaughan

V   1989 (July 7–31)
Bobbie Bailey
* Larry Bramon
Don Brooks
Dan Callahan, M.D.
Brandon Cotton
Doug Epps
Pat Epps

Neil Estes
Steve Felker
Doug Franks
Fafnir "Iceman" Frostason
Bob Harless
* Anna Henriquez
Addi Hermannsson
Kyle Jackson

Gil Lund
Lou Sapienza
Gordon Scott
* Harry Spencer
Jon Sveinsson
Richard Taylor
Norman Vaughan

VI
1990 (May 3–September 26)
Peter Austin
* Jack Belina
Don Brooks
Dan Callahan, M.D.
Bob Cardin
Andre Dekker
Doug Epps
Pat Epps
Neil Estes
Fafnir "Iceman" Frostason

Valdi Gudmundsson
* Jim Haney
Bob Harless
Addi Hermannsson
* Bill Ingram
Buzz Kaplan
Joe Longo
Pete Mallen
* Mark McSwiggen
* Ray Orton
Dirk Pohlmann
* Dick Plummer

Lou Sapienza
Gordon Scott
Jon Sveinsson
* Tony Seykora
Richard Taylor
* Frank Thomas
Ray Tousey
* Thomas A. Tubbs
* Carolyn Muegge-Vaughan
Norman Vaughan
George Wald
* R.T. "Bub" Way

PIZZAGALLI TEAM, 1990
Noel Adkins
F. J. Fortune, III
Kevin Hayes
John Heins

"Holmes" Holmes
Dan Maxwell
Angelo Pizzagalli
Gina Pizzagalli
Lisa Pizzagalli

Maria Pizzagalli
Remo Pizzagalli
Martin Quatt
Robin Sears
Robert "Wee Gee" Smith

VII
1992 (May 3–September 18)
* Cornelius Braun
Don Brooks
Dan Callahan, M.D.
Bob Cardin
* Pat Cardin
Pat Epps
Neil Estes
Tom Estes
Fafnir "Iceman" Frostason
John Fugedy
* Joey Hand
* Jim Haney
Bob Harless
* Todd Huvard
* Bill Ingram

Buzz Kaplan
Dave Kaufman
Sam Knaub
Gary Larkins
* Pete Mallen
* J. Bradley McManus
Thomas (T.K.) Mohr
* Terry Monmaney
Tony Pope
Lou Sapienza
Gordon Scott
Eddie Lou Shoffner
J. Roy Shoffner
Jorn Skyrud
Robert "Wee Gee" Smith
Wes Stricker, M.D.
Richard Taylor

* Richard Taylor, III
Bil Thuma
* O. Earl Toole
Norman Vaughan
George Wald
*R.T. (Bub) Way
* Jim Webber
Bart Wilder

*Ernie Bracy — ham radio operator maintained daily contact with GES ice-cap team by ham radio (W1BFA) in 1990 and 1992.

---

* These individuals were not on the expedition team, but either provided air transport or financial help, or in 1992, came to the ice cap for the day to celebrate the fiftieth anniversary.

David Hayes would like to thank the following.

Many people gave generously of their time and shared their memories during the preparation of this book. Some of them are named in the text, while others do not appear at all although their contributions have been no less significant. It is impossible to name everyone, but I would like to single out a number of individuals without whom this project would have been difficult, if not impossible.

Pat Epps and Richard Taylor made themselves available to me at all times and were unfailingly forthright about all aspects of the Greenland Expedition Society's quest for the Lost Squadron (as well as being hospitable hosts whenever I visited Atlanta). It was their energy and determination over more than a decade that made the eventual recovery of a historical aircraft possible.

Vivid accounts of several ice-cap expeditions were contained in the diaries, photographs and memories of two veteran expeditioners, Neil Estes and Gordon Scott. I am also indebted to Don Brooks and Norman Vaughan, who were unfailingly helpful, and to David Kaufman, for his detailed written and oral history of the 1992 expedition. Thanks to Jay Fiondella, who provided information and visual materials about non-GES efforts during the mid-1980s — especially the Winston Recovery Team expedition of 1983 — and to Russell Rajani, who also provided many pictures.

In addition to his supporting role in the history of Lost Squadron expeditions, Bil Thuma acted as an unofficial technical adviser on geophysical matters. I am grateful for his help.

The aircraft might still be under the ice if it weren't for the contributions of Roy Shoffner and Bob Cardin, who were instrumental to the success of the 1992 expedition. Their assistance to me was invaluable.

Piecing together events that happened more than half a century ago is always difficult. Fortunately, I received help from a number of surviving airmen who were involved in the 1942 forced landing on the ice cap. For sharing their memories and, in some cases, their private papers, I would like to thank Robert B. Wilson, Robert H. Wilson, Carl Rudder, Bill Bayless, Glenn E. Guoan and, especially, Brad McManus. Also thanks to Oran Earl Toole, the only surviving member of the rescue team.

Special thanks to Pat Epps's wife, Ann, and his daughter, Elaine, who acted as efficient archival consultants throughout this project and were particularly vigilant on the subject of misspellings.

Finally, I would like to acknowledge the people who made the writing of this book possible. My literary agent, Lee Davis Creal, has guided and supported me through the bad weather and uncertain communications of book publishing for the past seven years. As for the day-to-day mechanics of bringing the book together, I'm grateful to Ian R. Coutts for his skillful editing and droll sense of humor.

As always, I would like to thank my parents and, especially, Maya Gallus, whose personal and creative support is unquantifiable.

Madison Press Books would like to thank the following
for their contribution to the book.

Bobbie Bailey, a key player in the whole Lost Squadron story, who helped in a thousand different ways to bring this book into existence.

Peter Elek, who first brought the Lost Squadron story to Madison's attention, and helped smooth its transit from idea to finished book.

Hugh Morgan, who tracked down many rare pictures at the United States Air Force Museum and then printed those pictures for us. Eric Schulzinger of Lockheed and Alwyn T. Lloyd of Boeing, who supplied color and black and white pictures from their companies' collections. Thanks to Glenn E. Guoan, Brad McManus, Oran Earl Toole and R. B.

Wilson for lending us their precious personal World War II pictures. Thanks also to Cornelius Braun, Susan C. Epps, David Kaufman and Louis Sapienza for their many fine photographs and to Russell Rajani, Jay Fiondella and all the members of the GES who were kind enough to lend us their personal pictures. Thanks to Bil Thuma, who checked and rechecked diagrams.

Finally special thanks to the Greenwich Workshop, for arranging for two fine artists, Craig Kodera and William S. Phillips, to create paintings for this book. (For information on William S. Phillips's and Craig Kodera's limited-edition fine art prints, please call 1-800-243-4246.)

Picture and Illustration Credits

Every effort has been made to correctly attribute all material reproduced in this book. If any errors have unwittingly occurred, we will be happy to correct them in future editions.

Select Bibliography

Balchen, Bernt. *Come North With Me: An Autobiography*. London: Hodder & Stoughton, 1958.

Balchen, Colonel Bernt, with Major Corey Ford and Major Oliver La Farge. *War Below Zero*. Boston: Houghton Mifflin, 1944.

Banks, Michael. *Greenland*. Totowa, New Jersey: Rowman & Littlefield, 1975.

Beaver, Paul, ed. *Encylopedia of Aviation*. Hong Kong: Mandarin Publishers/Octopus Books, 1986.

Belina, John L. *Recovering Tomcat Flight*. Privately published, 1990.

Bracy, Ernest L. *From Here — The World*. Privately published, 1990.

———. *Highlights of 1992 Greenland Expedition*. Privately published, 1992.

Bright, Charles D., ed. *Historical Dictionary of the U.S. Air Force*. New York: Greenwood Press, 1992.

Brodie, Warren M. *The Lockheed P-38 Lightning*. Hiawassee, Georgia: Widewing Publications, 1991.

Caidin, Martin. *Air Force*. New York: Arno Press, 1980.

Carlson, William S. *Greenland Lies North*. New York: Macmillan, 1940.

———. *Lifelines Through the Arctic*. New York: Duell, Sloan & Pearce, 1962.

Cave, Hugh B. *Wings Across the World: The Story of the Air Transport Command*. New York: Dodd, Mead & Company, 1945.

Editorial staff of Air Classics Review. *P-38 Lightning Aces*. Canoga Park, California: Challenge Publications, 1993.

Ethell, Jeffrey L. *P-38 Lightning*. London: Jane's Publishing Company, 1983.

Goldbery, Alfred, ed. *A History of the United States Air Force, 1907-57*. New York: Arno Press, 1972.

Green, William. *Famous Bombers of the Second World War*. Garden City, New York: Doubleday & Company, 1975.

———. *Famous Fighters of the Second World War*. Garden City, New York: Doubleday & Company, 1976.

Judge, Henry, ed. *Oxford Illustrated Encyclopedia of the Physical World*. London: Oxford University Press, 1985.

McGraw-Hill *Encyclopedia of Science and Technology*. New York: McGraw-Hill, 1992.

Meyers, Robert A., ed. *Encyclopedia of Physical Science and Technology.* San Diego, California: Academic Press, 1992.

Mondey, David, ed. *International Encyclopedia of Aviation.* New York: Crown, 1977.

Mullins, John D. *Hello Spacebar, This is Springcap: A History of the 94th Fighter Squadron in World War II.* Kerrville, Texas: Hillside Cottage Publications, 1991.

O'Leary, Michael. *USAAF: Fighters of World War Two.* London: Bladford Press, 1986.

Parrish, Thomas, ed. *Simon and Schuster Encyclopedia of World War II.* New York: Simon & Schuster, 1978.

Reynolds, Pamela. *The P-38 Lightning.* Paducah, Kentucky: Turner Publishing Co., 1989.

Rossiter, Sean. *Legends of the Air: Aircraft, Pilots and Planemakers from the Museum of Flight.* Seattle, Washington: Sasquatch Books, 1990.

Royal Danish Ministry for Foreign Affairs. *Greenland.* 1961.

Thoren, Ragnar. *Picture Atlas of the Arctic.* Amsterdam: Elsevier Publishing Co., 1969.

Vaughan, Norman D., with Cecil B. Murphey. *With Byrd at the Bottom of the World.* Harrisburg, Pennsylvania: Stackpole Books, 1990.

Wheal, Elizabeth-Anne, and Stephen Pope and James Taylor. *A Dictionary of the Second World War.* London: Grafton Books, 1989.

INDEX

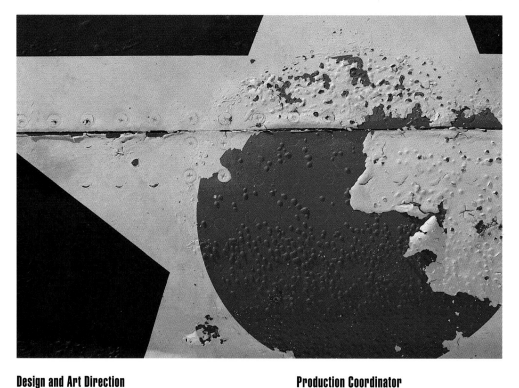

Design and Art Direction
Andrew Smith Graphics Inc.

Editorial Director
Hugh M. Brewster

Project Editor
Ian R. Coutts

Copy Editor
Shelley Tanaka

Production Director
Susan Barrable

Production Coordinator
Sandra L. Hall

Paintings
Craig Kodera, William S. Phillips

Maps and Diagrams
Jack McMaster

Color Separation
Colour Technologies

Printing and Binding
Butler & Tanner Ltd.

The Lost Squadron
was produced by Madison Press Books
under the direction of Albert E. Cummings